LIVING AT LIGHT SPEED

LIVING AT
LIGHT SPEED

Your Survival Guide to Life on
the Information Superhighway

Danny Goodman

RANDOM HOUSE

New York

CONTENTS

CONTENTS

INTRODUCTION

When, in the mid-1960s, I watched television commercials by big computer companies like Xerox, Wang, and IBM, I didn't have a clue about what they were trying to tell me. A common thread among these image-building ads was the movement of something called *information*. I recall animation showing a starlike speck of light racing down a path from New York to London, then halfway around the world to Tokyo. As a teenager in middle-class suburbia, I didn't have the faintest idea about what information could be, much less why anyone would be interested in moving it to various points around the world. I was more concerned about getting up in time for the school bus, plotting to get out of mowing the lawn, and memorizing age-old course material to get good grades to get into college. Even if I had had an inkling back then about what information was, I wouldn't have given it a second thought—figuring it belonged to the realm of giant computers and businesses that would never touch me.

Today that speck of light—information—is racing down a pathway that in some fashion is already connected to my home in more than one place. Your home, too. And probably your workplace as well. That pathway is now better known as a highway or superhighway, and the stuff that travels on it is called information or data. You cannot go one week of watching television news, listening to talk radio, or reading the newspaper without hearing about this *information superhighway*.

In fact, the popular media is doing a good job of confusing everyday folks about what the information superhighway is all about. One night not long ago, I saw a respected television news personality in San Francisco doing a ten-second teaser for the upcoming eleven o'clock news; his approach made my hair stand on end. With his jacket off and sleeves rolled up to show us how hard he was digging out the news for us, he was seated at a newsroom desk, beside a desktop personal computer. As the studio camera came alive, he warned us that the information superhighway was coming. At eleven, he claimed, the news program would tell us everything we needed to know about buying a personal computer.

Huh? Hello? Never mind the ludicrous proposition that a two-minute newscast could equip anyone with sufficient knowledge to buy a computer—more important, was he actually telling me that a personal computer was all I needed to know about the information superhighway?

When I saw that tiny ad, I hoped that the majority of the viewing audience was in the kitchen or bathroom during this commercial break; or that they would watch the program on videotape the next day and zap the entire commercial block; or that they had channel-surfed their way to another station. But of course I knew that untold thousands of viewers must have seen that teaser and were left with a perhaps indelible impression that "personal computer" equals "information superhighway."

The experience sensitized me to the mass media's abuse of the information superhighway buzz phrases. Daily newspapers, business publications, magazines, and the broadcast media had jumped onto the information superhighway bandwagon—without jumping onto the highway or taking the requisite driver training. The term *information superhighway*, and its derivatives, became the dumping ground for every story that touched on cellular telephones, cable television, video games, phone and cable companies—and, oh yes, personal computers. Proliferation of the term also brought along sad attempts at cleverness with every possible metaphor for anything connected with the information superhighway: roadside stands, passing lanes, rest stops, potholes, and road kill, to name several.

Perhaps it's unfair to place too much blame on the media. For the most part news media are simply reporting the tidbits and predictions coming out of the telecommunications, cable, computer, and entertainment industries. To have a chance of getting any exposure, these corporate plans, dreams, and business deals must sound good. The truth, however, is that most of the news these days is not about the information superhighway's effects on our lives, but about how companies are aligning with each other, falling out with each other, buying each other, selling each other, and spending big bucks on the pavement that will become the highway. Hearing the press conferences and reading the press releases, how can anyone get an impression other than that the world will be a utopian interconnected globe?

Yet through all the forecasts and visions, I can't help but get the feeling that we, the consumers of this supposedly life-enhancing technology, are being left out of the picture except for the money that is currently tucked away in our wallets. Despite the rosy pictures presented by the players, the highway and everything that flows on it won't magically appear, paid for by a fairy godmother. This is big business. Whether the technology reaches us and members of our family at home, work, or school, the costs are being met by dollars coming from our pockets and purses. We may see the cost directly in the form of a monthly bill for services we access on the highway, or it may be built into prices we pay for virtually any product that is available or advertised on the highway.

There's nothing wrong with paying for these things. All we really should expect in return is value for our money. And as with any purchase or trade, it's not always easy to recognize when we're getting good value for our dollar.

That's what this book is about: arming you as a concerned citizen with the knowledge to discriminate between hype and fact and avoid getting ripped off by premature or unfulfillable promises. Valuable and usable parts of the information superhighway are already in place, so it's also important to know whether you should become a participant now…and how to do so wisely. At the same time, we must learn how to keep the highway technology from being used against us by government, commercial, and individual interests—a genuine threat in light of the ease with which computers will be scoping out traffic on the highway.

But perhaps the most important message I hope you receive from this book is that all of us, as consumers (or potential consumers) of "stuff" coursing its way along the information superhighway, must play a role in molding the highway and its content into an empowering technology. If we can't use this technology to become better friends, parents, teachers, students, bosses, employees, and citizens, then these great technology and sociology experiments will have been for naught.

As high-tech communications links reach out to our homes, workplaces, and schools within the next several decades or so, our day-to-day lives are destined to change at a pace that will make the 1980s seem as distant as the 1940s do today. Let's do our best to encourage these ventures to empower rather than enslave us.

CHAPTER ONE

Ready or Not, Here Comes the I-Way

If it were possible to listen directly to digital signals—the normally silent on and off pulses that flow through practically everything electronic—you'd know what to listen for as the information superhighway rumbles ever closer to your personal world. Whether you like it or not, even if you haven't a clue about what it is, the highway is coming: to your workplace, your community school system, and your home.

Sound like a threat? Perhaps, but as you'll learn here, hooking up to the highway may benefit you much more than pretending it doesn't exist. How strong the links are to you in your home, work, and family life, and how much benefit you derive from these links, will be largely up to you. But first you need to know what's "out there." *Living at Light Speed* will take a look at the options available to you as you acquaint yourself with the future known as the information superhighway.

The Highway as Metaphor

Early discussion about the information superhighway made use of the highway metaphor to compare the effort needed to wire America with that of paving America with interstate highways, begun in the 1950s. And it's true that great parallels can be drawn between automobile and information highways.

Perhaps the most important similarity is that both kinds of highways are merely the links between people and places. By themselves, roadways contribute nothing to society. They're no more than inanimate concrete and asphalt ribbons. But place some vehicles carrying goods and people on those roads, and suddenly we have commerce, travel, and interactive exchanges among people. The same is true for an information highway. In its purest form, the highway is nothing more than the physical connection between people and places. But when we start shuffling stuff around that web of wires, glass fibers, and radio links—*then* we stand a chance to grow and prosper.

So, the auto and info highways *do* bear a certain conceptual resemblance. But it's also important to realize that some crucial elements distinguish the two endeavors.

For example, the imperative that drove the interstate highway system had little to do with personal commuting patterns or driving to Grandma's house for Christmas: military defense was the motivating factor. The idea was to create a system of high-speed roadways that would allow for rapid deployment of mobile missile launchers across this great land. In the event of nuclear attack, trucks bearing retaliatory nuclear missiles could race to areas out of harm's way and destroy the other half of the world. As often happens with grandiose projects established in the name of national security, the interstate highway system became a magnet for huge amounts of government cash. Thus, with 90 percent of the tab for building these highways covered by the federal government, our interstates were built and the system nearly complete forty years later. Most interstate highways remain free to anyone with a motor vehicle (although our taxes pay for much of the maintenance).

In contrast with this great example of government munificence, the job of wiring America for the information highway, according to Capitol Hill, belongs with private industry. And since there isn't much money in the government's revenue stream to pay for this technology, the only way to get the highway built quickly is to provide the right kinds of incentives to private industry, such as reduced regulation and open market competition—incentives that won't have to show up as line items in the federal budget. Of course this means that as consumers we will be faced with having to make choices that might be made for us if the government took over the job. But no one said living in a capitalistic democracy was easy! Freedom of choice is as much a responsibility as it is a right.

Another potential distinction between the auto and info highways is that the former connotes a multilane road that serves thousands of individual users each day. Roads are shared resources we all use. The information highway is far more ambitious in its reach. A paved highway merely links towns, cities, or whole regions with one another; the information highway, on the other hand, also provides access to the side streets and driveways leading straight to our doors. Of course, less traffic flows into and out of an individual home than from one coast to another, which will affect the breadth of the two kinds of connections, but by and large, implementing the information superhighway to its full potential means "repaving" virtually the entire country.

The Telecommunications Continuum

As innovative as the information highway may sound, it is important to recognize its role in the evolution of telecommunications. Oddly enough, much of what is happening on the business side of the information highway of the twenty-first century echoes events in communications technologies dating back to the commercial telegraph of the 1840s. Moreover, some lessons in the history of telecommunications will inevitably shape the adoption of the new technologies.

Telegraphy

The spread of wire telegraphy in the United States received a big boost not from the federal government, but from private industry. While the U.S. government did sponsor and pay for a trial stretch of Samuel F. B. Morse's telegraph line in the mid-1840s (linking Baltimore, Maryland, with Washington, D.C.), the job of wiring communities together was left to private telegraph companies. Much of the wiring at first ran along railroad rights-of-way, because the railroads themselves used the telegraph service to communicate with railroad stations and yards along the lines. While businesses and consumers eventually began to rely on the telegraph for speedy messaging, the various types of long-short, dot-dash codes generated with a telegraph key—the user interface of telegraphy—was left to the specialists. To send a message, you went down to the telegraph office; to receive a message, a local messenger physically delivered a transcribed copy.

"Watson..."

Like the telegraph, the telephone also went through transformations in its purpose. Its inventor, Alexander Graham Bell, envisioned the telephone as a broadcast device—essentially a wired precursor to radio. News, public speeches, and music would be piped into everyone's home. In the United States, however, person-to-person communications became the telephone's raison d'être. As long-distance lines spread in the 1880s and 1890s, businesses were quick to see the potential of instant, live communication with colleagues and customers. Initially, telephone connections among people required going through a human operator, who, using a massive switchboard, literally connected the wires between callers. That led some visionaries at the time to predict that for every household to have a telephone, the country would need on the order of ten million switchboard operators.

A new technology, called *switching*, not only made a giant change in the advances of telephony for consumers, but continues today to play a role in the information highway landscape. Automatic switches (originally electromechanical, now electronic) allowed users themselves to effect a connection by dialing a phone number. As the rotary phone dial whirred back counterclockwise, the phone sent pulses to the automatic switching office, where electromechanical relays and switches connected caller and receiver in a matter of seconds, without any human assistance. Modern tone dialing phones do the same with audio signals, which are interpreted at the phone switching office by its electronic switches. Thus the ability today to connect any two users on a network in a substantially private connection, while hardly a startling innovation, is of fundamental importance to advanced services expected to become available on the information superhighway.

Cutting the Cord

Based originally on the business-oriented telegraphy model, radio originated in the mid-1890s as a way of sending telegraph messages without being restricted to a wired path. The first wireless devices transmitted information no more complex than a crackle of static, which when triggered by a telegraph key could replicate the long and short codes used by telegraph operators. Crude, perhaps, but for ships at sea this was a godsend when the alternative was no communication at all with land.

Even as the technology progressed over the years, allowing radio waves to convey sound, application remained primarily commercial. World War I stimulated a certain paranoia in government about allowing free access to the airwaves (and communications with naval ships); eventually the U.S. Navy seized all commercial radio stations and shut down the private amateur stations as well. After the war, sensitivity to the powers of radio still ran high in Washington, where the State Department endorsed an effort to keep all U.S. broadcasting under the navy's control. A vocal outcry, primarily from those already involved with radio in the public sector, put an end to the navy's monopoly but also—inadvertently—fostered the creation of a public monopoly, Radio Corporation of America (RCA). RCA was not a neophyte operation, having boosted its market power by acquiring American Marconi and its wireless messaging network. Along with the company came a young radio operator, David Sarnoff, who in 1916 suggested that consumers would one day want to buy "radio music boxes." Although Sarnoff's vision, dismissed as harebrained, was difficult to grasp with no professional radio broadcast stations in operation, the idea gained steam after the overwhelming success of the first licensed radio station, KDKA, in Pittsburgh (1920). By 1924 nearly 5 percent of U.S. households had radios, with hundreds of stations popping up all over the country in search of the advertising dollar.

A key point in broadcast radio's success in its earliest days was that the medium was delivering something unavailable elsewhere. KDKA's first broadcast consisted of live election returns for the 1920 presidential race between Warren G. Harding and James M. Cox. The radio provided a timeliness that newspapers were hard-pressed to convey. Information played a pivotal role initially (offering daily information for farmers, for example), but entertainment gradually drew huge audiences, which began to consider a radio receiver as a basic household need, even during the Depression.

Radiovision

Unlike the telegraph, telephone, and radio, which were conceived as a means of offering person-to-person messaging, television sprang full-blown as a medium for information and entertainment targeted for mass consumption. Today, the money to pay for the television broadcast infrastructure derives largely from advertisers (for free broadcasts), from consumers (premium, commercial-free television channels such as HBO), and from a combination of consumer and advertiser (commercial-laden programming on secondary channels available only via cable systems). The government funds only a small portion of what comes across our TV sets in the form of grants to public television stations.

Sea Changes

At the very beginning of all of these communications technologies, few consumers envisioned how their lives would change once these services became widely available and affordable. Person-to-person messaging through telegraphy, telephone, and radio improved radically in speed and quality; later developments in commercial radio and then television brought timely information and new types of entertainment into our homes. With the exception of television, these technologies usually had to prove themselves in the business world before they became sociologically accepted and then affordable by mass production.

The information superhighway is following in that tradition. Businesses now frequently rely on electronic messaging and electronic exchange of documents. Videoconferencing equipment purchased from a mail-order catalog can be added to virtually any personal computer. Once these technologies are accepted as routine in the workplace, demand for home versions won't be far behind.

Communications companies today seem more impatient, however, not only in getting the information superhighway hooked up to our homes and pockets, but in defining the types of information—the *content*—that will make the highways useful. To attract customers, the content on the highway must be compelling. Why else would we discard traditional messaging, information, and entertainment media? We won't make a big change in our lives just for an incremental improvement. Once the infrastructure is there, speculators predict, the content providers will rise to the occasion. It has happened before in other related areas—look at the proliferation of desktop publishing now that anyone can buy an easy-to-use, high-resolution video personal computer and affordable laser printers. So the potential is there.

The First Highway

While the notion of a highway for information sounds like something a Silicon Valley company would dream up for an ad campaign, its source was an unlikely player in an unlikely place—then Congressman Albert Gore, Jr., in Washington, D.C. What's so unlikely about this source? First, the information highway is a long-term project that requires great technical expertise to complete: the idea of a member of Congress having a vision beyond the next election is a wonder by itself. But that Gore had absorbed the required technical expertise to debate intelligently about a highly complex subject is even more amazing, given the confines of a typical political role.

In 1991, then Senator Al Gore wrote:

> To realize the full benefit of the information age, we need to take the next step: high-speed networks must be built that tie together millions of computers, providing capabilities that we cannot even imagine....For almost 15 years, I have been working to change federal policy so that as a nation we will invest in the critical infrastructure of information superhighways. (Al Gore, "Infrastructure for the Global Village," *Scientific American*, September 1991.)

The article in which these words appeared suggested the highway be built largely with government funding to ensure consistency and compatibility across the network. Private industry, however, stepped forward to discourage a "federally funded 'backbone,'" instead advocating an openly competitive environment for building the highway. Fast-moving technology companies feared, for one, that a government bureaucracy would inhibit application of new technologies as they came along. Senator Gore listened closely.

As vice president, Mr. Gore has accelerated his efforts to wire America (under the National Information Infrastructure banner) and to allow all parties equal access to our homes. Some of this requires undoing government regulations that were designed originally to save consumers from predatory, anticompetitive practices. Now is a good time to reevaluate these regulations, because the business and technology climates have changed dramatically in the last few years—largely because of the prominence of the high-tech players in the U.S. economy.

In 1994, Congress came within inches of passing a law that would have fundamentally changed the way utility providers—telephone, cable TV, and electrical companies, to name a few—conduct their business. The ultimate goal of this legislation was to eventually give these industries the freedom to provide access and content to any style of information and communication services.

While legislation has stalled, cable and phone companies are pushing ahead through the courts and regulatory agencies to achieve the same results. The bottom line, however, is that a large segment of the country will soon experience a significant change in the current, frustratingly monopolistic delivery of electronic services to the home.

With that gift to consumers comes a price, however—competition may make our personal decisions more difficult. Before all this competitive talk, life was easy: when you moved into a new home in a new community, you called the phone company for phone service, the cable company for television, and the electric company for power. Within the next several years, these reassuring monoliths will disappear, as competitors for all utilities (including electricity) vie for individual household business. If you want to find out what may be available on competing systems, you'll have to check them out yourself. More than likely, however, the services will know you've moved, based on change-of-address data supplied by cooperating service providers from your previous location, and you'll be bombarded with offers from each carrier. Too much of a good thing? Perhaps. The alternative, however, is what exists in most communities today: one service provider for each kind of service, charging what the monopolistic market or government regulations will bear.

Bits and Bits and Bits

American consumers have long been familiar with such high-tech toys as personal computers, the wired and cellular telephone, and cable television. Why then, is there a sudden interest in funneling all this technology into our daily lives via the information superhighway? The answer begins with a concept that dates back decades: electronically transmitted *digital* information.

The evolution and implementation of digital information have taken many paths, but the critical path passes through the first electronic computers, such as the ENIAC, which came into service just after World War II. Among the characteristics of a classic digital computer is that all signals that flow through its circuits represent numbers. For example, a number might correspond to a letter of the alphabet or a simple instruction that the computer carries out. A few generations after the ENIAC, computers processed numbers that were represented in the binary (base 2) counting system, where a digit is either an "on" or "off" state, more commonly represented by the digits "1" and "0." The term *binary digit* was contracted into the word *bit*, which represented the smallest piece of raw data that a computer worked with. Later, common practice inside computers was to represent alphabetical characters, punctuation marks, and other symbols by a binary number that consisted of eight binary digits. For example, the binary number 01000001 converts to our more common decimal numbering system as the number 65. By industry convention, this value came to represent the capital letter "A."

From Waves to Bits

This is a long way to go to reach the fact that today virtually all computers work with information that is stored in binary digital format—*bits*. Even information that does not start out as bits, such as your speaking voice, can be converted to bits. To do this, a computer takes tens of thousands of instantaneous samples for each second of the voice wave that reaches a microphone and converts each sample reading to a number. To play back the recording, another computer converts those sampled numbers into audio that plays through a speaker. That's exactly the principle behind the digital audio compact disc, which a few years ago overtook the LP record as the music consumer's platter of choice.

Digital data has a number of benefits over the natural world's analog data. For example, an analog sound wave generated by a tree falling in the woods grows weaker and more distorted as it travels through air from the point of the fall. An analog tape recorder may capture the sound, but in the recording process the wave loses some of its original shape, as mechanical forces (primarily friction of the tape moving past the recording head) interfere with the wave. Making additional copies or transmitting the sound over the radio also reduces fidelity to the original wave, especially as distance and other factors affect the wave. But if that sound is converted at its source into bits, it is easier to reproduce and retransmit the streams of 1s and 0s on tape, disk, or radio signal with 100 percent accuracy. A copy can be compared mathematically against the original to ensure a perfect copy, even many generations distant.

The more complicated the data, however, the greater the number of bits required to represent the information. Plain text information is compact, because in its rawest form it takes only 8 bits to represent each character, numeral, and punctuation mark of any roman alphabet. But one second of high-fidelity sound to speak that letter would require 617,400 bits at today's lowest-fidelity CD quality (a 14-bit value for each of the 44,100 samples per second). One second of broadcast-quality color video requires more than 110 million bits.

The Bandwidth Factor

So, you may ask, how much digital information can actually reach me? Simple—the only limiting factor here is the number of *bits per second* (bps) that can flow through the conduit to your home. Great strides have been made in technologies of digital compression and decompression, all of which make it possible to convey information with fewer bits (the missing bits are reinserted at the receiving end, so the recipient sees as much of the same material transmitted by the sender as the compression math allows). Today's standard telephone line, which requires that digital signals first be converted to audio signals by a *modem*, permits up to 14,400 bits per second with reasonable reliability on a local call. A typical fax machine sends information at the rate of 9,600 bits per second. But these rates pale in comparison with the approximately 1 million bits per second (Mbps) needed to send a color television picture in its most compressed form.

Information highway services envisioned for our personal use require a much fatter conduit—a wider *bandwidth*—to accommodate the quantities of bits that make up a pleasant interactive experience, anything from home shopping to picking a movie to watch to looking up an encyclopedia entry. Phone companies have been slowly adopting one possible digital connection to homes and offices, called Integrated Services Digital Network (ISDN).

Designed by Bell Labs in the 1970s to take into account existing phone wiring to homes, ISDN conveys information strictly as digital data, rather than the analog voice data you currently get via your household phone jack. Typical specifications for a consumer ISDN line feature two 64 kbps (kilobits, or 1000 bits, per second) data lines, plus one 1,500 bps control line. Using just one 64 kbps line for on-line data retrieval of text and static art is passable by today's standards, but any live video or animation appears jerky, because far fewer frames of video can be sent each second compared with broadcast-quality video. Even combining the two 64 kbps channels doesn't help much.

Business videoconferencing is starting to use ISDN, but in a more robust setting. A typical corporate ISDN installation includes twenty-three data lines (at 64 kbps each) plus one control line. With the right equipment on both ends of a videoconference call, the twenty-three data lines can be bunched together to achieve sufficient bandwidth for high-quality color video sent at nearly 1.5 Mbps.

At the moment, then, a considerable gap exists between business and consumer implementations of ISDN, even in communities where service is available. Moreover, ISDN standards were established so long ago that today's dreams for the information superhighway outrun ISDN's current consumer-level capabilities.

Optical Dreams

Fiber-optic cables—literally thin glass tubes that transmit digital data as light pulses—while physically thin, are digitally fat, capable of passing millions of bits per second. Massive long-distance carrier fiber-optic network installations over the past several years have already vastly improved the audio quality of long-distance calls. Between most major cities, it is virtually impossible these days to distinguish a long distance from a local call based on the quality of the sound coming through the telephone handset. Even local phone companies are replacing copper wire with fiber-optic lines in the course of normal replacement, because the fiber-optic lines are cheaper than wire.

Fiber-optic links are what the phone companies have in mind for linking schools to the information superhighway. Since hundreds of computers could be connected during the day, it's essential that the conduit allow as many simultaneous connections as possible. Fiber-optic delivery to the home on a universal basis will take longer to complete, until consumers demonstrate demand for more bits than broadband cable or ISDN can deliver.

When Worlds Converge

With digital data becoming a kind of lingua franca (even if the precise format of the data requires software inside a computer, set-top box, or handheld personal digital assistant (PDA) to decode and display the information), all content-oriented services are rushing to make sure their data is ready to flow on the information superhighway. Practically every second of commercially recorded music is recorded digitally. Many feature films are being digitized and distributed now on laser discs (and soon to theaters via phone wires). Although an agonizingly huge and expensive undertaking, libraries are digitizing their collections—text and illustrations—for electronic preservation and distribution. A number of newspapers and magazines, whose contents are assembled in digital format prior to paper publication, are currently available via on-line services, albeit only in text format for now. A number of highly regarded reference works—dictionaries and encyclopedias—have been digitized for distribution on CD-ROM (compact disc-read only memory) discs for use on personal computers. Many telephone companies provide telephone answering services at their central offices, enabling callers to leave audio messages whose contents are stored in the phone companies' computers in digital format.

A primary benefit of having much of the world's information in digital format is that all of it can be sent over digital data connections—the very foundation of the information superhighway.

The "information" part of the information superhighway is somewhat presumptuous. In truth, the highway is simply a digital data conduit. Bits of raw data from millions of sources stream through the conduit in a sequence of ones and zeros. That data becomes information only when it is decoded and its original meaning is restored at the receiving end. A term frequently used to connote the indiscriminate meshing of vastly different information into digital data is *digital convergence*. More specifically, digital convergence refers to the fact that when content is reduced to a stream of bits directed at customers, the various boundaries among specific industries—computing, publishing, entertainment, and communications, for example—seem to blur. The boundaries blur, too, when the bits are decoded at the customer's data "receiver"—either a personal computer, set-top box, or PDA. Traditional expectations of receiving certain kinds of information only from a particular source or played through a specific device may disappear. Video programming, for example, could become available from a utility company that used to provide only telephone service; the local cable TV company may provide a link to an on-line computer service that lets you read this week's *Time* magazine or send e-mail to your child at college; compact-disc-quality music may play through a stereo-equipped personal computer after being received directly from a digital broadcast satellite.

The Conduits

It's difficult these days to go through a full week of daily newspapers without reading about some cable, phone, electric, or other high-tech company forming an alliance with other players on the information superhighway. A lot of jockeying these days has to do with establishing conduits across the country and directly into your home or pocket. But all this probably means little to you as a consumer— until it connects your immediate world with the highway.

One distinguishing feature of the information super-highway is that the on-ramps will not be the same around the country. In fact, what is available to your home, office, or school will depend on the regional and local companies who build those ramps. Few communities will have the same number or width of conduits available for home and commercial use. Each geographical parcel—equivalent to a telephone exchange area or a cable TV company's cover-age—will implement its on-ramps differently, and the num-ber of ramps will also vary widely. You may have experienced this phased-in methodology for advanced call-ing features on your telephone. Some exchanges within your area code get the services before others, because the phone company has to install lots of equipment over an ex-tended period to equip the entire region for all services.

Even when a system provider completes installation in the region, the available quantity of what can flow through the conduit will vary from provider to provider, just as cable TV channel capacity varies from community to community today. Moreover, don't be startled by the appearance in your community of new system providers who weren't there be-fore. The electric utility could be one.

Many information enthusiasts are unaware that electric utilities have long had fiber-optic cables strung across their power grids (running along the high-capacity power lines). The utilities use only a fraction of the cable's capac-ity to monitor and control their own systems, so some could easily extend the network to the neighborhood or home level itself, or even license its data rights-of-way to other highwaynauts.

Another user–information highway conduit is the wireless connection. Today's two-way wireless digital data networks operate largely on the backs of existing wireless voice networks like cellular telephones and commercial dispatching. Other networks in the planning stages include satellite systems that will offer access to anything digital from virtually any spot on the planet that can see sky overhead. Some corporate office buildings are equipped today with wireless networks that allow employees to access corporate information from notebook computers—*wherever* those employees happen to be.

Initially, wireless data connections will cost more than wired connections: wireless networks are new, often require frequency spectrum allocations from the Federal Communications Commission, and are very costly to get up and running. Early users of the service will bear the higher costs of the convenience provided by wireless connections. Typically, business users will benefit most, since a significant percentage of workers (white and blue collar) have high-mobility requirements. But most wireless devices, such as the Motorola Envoy personal communicator, will contain a connector for hooking up to a wired network when the user can access a standard phone line (the incentive to use the wired network for noncritical communications will be its comparatively lower cost).

Still, the portable cellular telephone taught us an interesting lesson. Even though the first portables were large and expensive ($4,000 was not unusual), business users on the go became hooked on the convenience. Eventually, however, as manufacturing costs diminished with increased volume and advancing technology (fewer parts were required), the market broadened. Mobile homemakers, who spend a great deal of time in the car as chauffeurs and personal shoppers found cellular phones convenient for keeping tabs on their equally mobile family. We can't forget that as a security device—calling 911 in any emergency—the portable cellular phone has proven to be a lifesaver as well as a comfort on the streets. I am strongly convinced that future generations of portable, personal communicator devices will be inexpensive enough to enable every member of a family to have one to stay in touch with each other and friends throughout the day.

Conduits, then, will come in two forms: wired and wireless. The wires can range from the decades-old twisted-pair telephone wire to wider bandwidth copper cable to data-gushing fiber-optic cable. Wireless data—which ultimately reaches a wired system somewhere in its travel between sender and receiver—may come from anyplace in the ether. The less you have to worry about where it comes from, the more engaging the connection will be.

What's Traveling the Highway

If, as we've determined, the highway is carrying only bits of data, what kinds of information do these bits turn into once they reach us? Even after all the business alliances and engineering advances have paved the on-ramps to our homes, desks, or pockets, the billions of dollars spent in the process mean absolutely nothing without meaningful stuff to make the journey. Our only reason for wanting to travel the highway should be what's on it, not that it's there.

For the foreseeable future, the highway will lure us with three service categories: messaging, information, and entertainment. Each category covers a broad selection of individual services, although it is unlikely that we would use all services on the same device in the same part of our home, school, or office, even if we were attracted to all three categories. Throughout the remainder of this book, when I speak of all three categories, I will often refer to them as a group by the acronym MIE. This is not an industry standard; it's just something I dreamed up.

Messaging

To my way of thinking, messaging is one of the most compelling reasons humans should participate in the information superhighway. "Messaging" includes electronic mail as well as electronic bulletin board services that create what many call *virtual communities* among on-line computer users. Both kinds of messaging involve delayed or time-shifted connections between people. A third kind of messaging, increasingly popular on commercial services, involves live conferences, in which participants (today mostly via typed keyboard exchanges) converse live as a group or ask questions of a special guest—like a cocktail party or discussion group at which dozens of people see what the conversation is all about. Messaging is a compelling application for the information highway, because it keeps us in touch with other humans—family members, business associates, close friends, and others with similar interests. Rather than distancing highway riders from each other, the highway potentially brings them closer together.

Information

By far the least defined attraction to the highway is information—knowledge published and made available in digital format. That includes information published not only by traditional sources, but by individuals who have knowledge to share with others. Among the most common ideas for information that consumers would access on the highway are encyclopedias, news, weather, stock quotes, airline schedules, and government documents. Existing commercial services offer information of this type today, although they are limited primarily to textual presentations. But audio and visual information should also be included in this category: historical newsreel footage, audio recordings of commencement speeches given by prominent (and not-so-prominent) people, how-to videos, and other instructional material, whether targeted for the local elementary school, adult continuing education, or job retraining.

Business users are becoming the first avid superhighway travelers to take advantage of electronically published information, especially for travel information. Students and academicians comb libraries of information to assist in research without having to visit a library. Consumer enthusiasm for information will focus first around personal interests, as library-style adjuncts to the virtual communities that grow up around messaging. Beyond that, information providers will have to find ways of engaging users in information, aiming first at convenience and time-shifting factors, such as those inherent in electronic shopping. From a content point of view, this may be the single most difficult challenge ahead for companies that want to entice us onto their on-ramps. I'll have more to say about this in Chapter 5.

Entertainment

We're already plugged into electronic entertainment, primarily at home and during off hours, so if the superhighway can enhance our entertainment experiences, we may want to hasten access to an on-ramp. Without connecting to any highway, video and computer games already present plenty of action and strategy challenges for a variety of age groups within a household (including adults). Music and video consume the bulk of entertainment time and dollars at home. Perhaps the highway can provide a wider selection, offering the equivalent of several video rental store collections on an on-screen menu, available for immediate rental with just the touch of a few keys. And, lest we forget, reading is also entertainment for enough folks to keep bookstores comfortably in business. The information superhighway is reaching even the stodgy publishing industry as it gropes for ways to maintain a presence in the future.

To summarize, then, the data superhighway will offer messaging, information, and entertainment, all of which will reach individuals by wire and air. Before we begin to imagine how these technologies will change us, let's take a look at how today's comparatively crude implementations have already changed us.

CHAPTER TWO

Wagon Trails Transform a Civilization

Today's telecommunications infrastructure is to the information superhighway as wagon trails were to the interstate highway system. Everything has to start someplace.

As crude as America's early transcontinental wagon trails were, they opened up the continent to settlement that couldn't even be imagined some decades earlier. Today's electronic wagon trails, some of whose routes date back to the end of the nineteenth century, also transformed the world of MIE. Limiting our scope to just the past ten years, the basic telephone, cable, and wireless conduits—in concert with advances in equipment that connects to them—have transformed modern society. Most of the changes occurred while you weren't watching. The depth and suddenness of those changes in recent years teach valuable lessons about what to expect once the superhighway and its attendant pieces are in place.

Ancient Conduits

Phone Wires

While it's true that 98 percent of households in the United States are served today by telephone lines, virtually every home telephone is connected to the phone company via the plain old telephone system (POTS), which uses one or two pairs of tiny wires to handle the very restricted requirements of analog voice communications. This wiring is still called *twisted-pair*, after the way telephone wires were originally strung (to keep pairs of wires together for ease of identification by phone installers). This wiring scheme hasn't changed much in nearly a century.

That's not to say that the telephone network has been stagnant; quite the contrary. All the money and effort, however, have gone into parts of the telephone system that you don't see—the switching networks, powerful computers at local phone company offices, satellite links in the sky, and high-capacity fiber-optic cable links that crisscross the country and the oceans. You may not "see" the results, but you do experience them. In the United States you reach the number you dialed virtually every time; voice quality has improved dramatically; and local phone companies offer services (such as call waiting, call forwarding, caller ID) that add value to the service you're used to. You didn't have to change your phone or your household wiring to take advantage of these new services. You could literally connect a 1930s vintage rotary-dial telephone to the line coming into your home and have it direct-dial around the globe (compare that to a ten-year-old personal computer software program that more than likely wouldn't even run on today's PCs). You would need tone dialing of more modern phones to access some of the newer computerized services and voice mail, but you could still use the old phone for its original purpose.

TV Cable

Cable television comes in all varieties, so it is difficult to draw generalities about the cable TV experience. Some systems seem as old as the hills that originally prevented valley residents from receiving broadcast TV signals from the distant city serving the area. The first cable systems in the late 1940s were built by appliance dealers in signal-isolated towns. By putting a master antenna atop a nearby mountain and connecting it via coaxial cable to each household in the town, the dealer created a market for television sets that would otherwise not be there, no matter how many channels were broadcast from the faraway metropolis.

Today cable reaches about 60 percent of U.S. households. Some of the regions not served by cable are rural areas, where the cost of stringing cable to one farmhouse that extended for miles around would be prohibitive for both the cable operator and the homeowner. In other parts of the country the traditional broadcast system is enhanced by a wireless cable system, whereby traditional cable channels are broadcast to customers who rent set-top receiver/converter units.

For the most part, however, cable television installations send signals in one direction: from the cable company office to all subscribers. A handful of more advanced systems employ normally unused capacity on the cable for simple signals passing back from the subscriber to the cable office. Communication back to the office has been used for subscribers to sign up for pay-per-view movies and other special events (like championship boxing matches). The more common way for cable subscribers to communicate with the cable office is via telephone, usually a voice call to a human operator.

Channel capacities of cable systems also vary widely across the country. A surprising number of older systems are limited to approximately forty channels, including the local broadcast channels. When you take away the premium movie channels (HBO, Showtime, and so on) and mandatory local access channel, there is strong competition for comparatively few slots by dozens of specialty cable channels that are fed to local cable companies via satellite and fiber-optic cable. The cable company serving my community, for example, is forever juggling channel allocations, even sharing some channels. For instance, channel 30 (today, at least) airs Nickelodeon during the day and switches to A&E at 5:00 P.M.

More modern systems provide a wider range of cable selections, including extra local information channels that display text messages about local weather and community activities. There is plenty of spare capacity on newer systems to accommodate more program sources. The differences among system capacities is not in the physical cable that touches our homes, but in all other parts of the system at the cable company office and other black boxes hanging from the utility poles between the office and our homes. The physical cable is capable of handling lots of channels, provided the cable company has the wherewithal to send them.

The Airwaves

Existing wireless conduits have a number of implementations, each of which plays a role in a different segment of daily life. Radio and television broadcasting perform their primary jobs of providing information and entertainment for a wide range of listeners and viewers within the broadcast area.

Hidden from view on TV channels and from hearing on FM radio station frequencies, however, are an increasing number of digital signals that are used for enhanced entertainment services, close captioning for the hearing impaired, and business communications. In all cases these are one-way signals, from a central source to a distributed audience. That's not to say that the signals are "read" by everyone with a device to interpret them. For example, some one-way text messaging services (acting like paging services) send the signals to everyone within range; but the messages are coded so that only the receiver with a specific address bothers to store and display the message for the user.

The two-way wireless conduit has already been flooded with the cellular telephone. While wireless voice and, more recently, digital data are simply cordless extensions to the wired telephone world, they are playing a major role in shaping our lifestyles in the immediate years ahead—information superhighway or not.

The Gear and Services That Changed the World

Like the paved roads on a map, existing conduits are merely facilitators—the infrastructure available to any takers. Even with the mere wagon-trail-like pathways we've had at our disposal, a number of life-changing communications technologies have reached the desks, homes, and hands of millions of people in North America (and elsewhere, but I'm staying close to home for now). Engineers, marketers, and dreamers saw opportunities along those pathways and created products and services that took advantage of the infrastructure as it existed. Some failed, while others succeeded. Those that succeeded produced revenue streams and jobs, and they also changed the way modern society behaves—at the same time changing our expectations for future technology, whether we like it or want it or not.

How will we adapt to the information superhighway? Let's take a look at the recent history of our experiences on the information wagon trails.

Voice Mail and Answering Machines

How quickly attitudes about some technologies change! Ten years ago, answering machines were almost universally despised by the general public. Early adopters who bought machines, especially for the home, experienced plenty of empty messages, as callers would listen to the outgoing message and then either freeze or hang up because of "that damned machine." Some enterprising companies developed lines of humorous prerecorded outgoing messages to try to make callers feel more relaxed. Machine owners who recorded their own messages often went out of their way to encourage or beg the caller to leave a message.

Today, on the other hand, it's more common to be disappointed when someone *doesn't* have a machine (the phone just rings and rings) or a voice mail system on which you can leave a message. What happened in the interim?

Without any scientific research to back up my hypothesis, I believe that those who left a message—perhaps out of desperation at first—quickly learned that doing so accomplished more than hanging up. In fact, recording a message accomplishes a couple of important tasks.

First, by leaving a message, you can often begin a transaction—an information exchange—without having actually to reach the recipient. In other words, if you simply leave a message asking the person to call you because you need some information, you end up wasting valuable time by having the person initiate the search only *after* he or she returns your call. On the other hand, if you leave a message that explains in detail what you need, the person calling you back can do so with the information at hand. In the course of two telephone calls, you have accomplished what would take no fewer than three. And if you aren't available to receive the information when the person calls, your machine can catch it for you, eliminating yet another call in the transaction. An information exchange that could take days of telephone tag (each party leaving messages asking the other to call) can be completed in a matter of hours. It may sound like a cold transaction—two people communicating without truly talking to each other—but the currency of exchange is still the human voice. It's as if you're talking to the person, but they can't speak to you; or someone is talking to you, but you cannot interrupt. You can still exchange the same pleasantries and thank-yous, but it's just not a real-time transaction. This can (and does) happen even when the people have never spoken to each other before. A well-worded introduction by the initiating party is often all that is necessary to make the connection and set the transaction in motion.

Related to this issue of "speaking" to the person, even if not in real time, is the issue of accuracy. Most of us have experienced the frustration of "message corruption": leaving detailed messages with secretaries, assistants, receptionists, hotel operators, and human answering services, only to learn that they reached the recipient in less than satisfactory condition. Using your own voice to leave the message ensures the recipient will hear exactly what you want him or her to hear. Of course, that doesn't guarantee the *meaning* will get across, but the odds are better.

A second, more devious reason people adapt well to deferred voice messaging is that it is a perfectly acceptable way of shifting responsibility for something that's too hot to handle. You have probably been the victim in an incident in which a caller lights the fuse of a bomb, places it gently on your answering tape, and then hangs up. Time goes by, you return to listen to your messages, the bomb goes off in your face, and you've got to clean up the mess. Repeat victims of this mayhem may have to plant a few bombs of their own in return. While you may not know who the caller is, you can sometimes tell when you have averted a bombing: you are able to pick up the phone when it rings, and the caller hangs up because the machine didn't answer.

An important aspect of the success of voice mail and answering machines repeats itself in many successful business-related technologies. With a machine or computer answering our telephones for us, we defy time and schedules. Catching people when they're in their offices or at home is no longer a factor. You leave messages when it's convenient for you; the recipients hear messages when it's convenient for them. We can live by our own clocks and still get plenty of work done.

Electronic Mail

Electronic mail (e-mail) is a common application in business and the research worlds of academia. For those who haven't been exposed to e-mail, the concept may seem mystifying, but it isn't, really. Electronic mail is just like it sounds: instead of creating a physical letter on a typewriter or through pen and paper, you type an e-mail message on a computer keyboard. The message is then sent to an electronic version of the central post office, where every participant has a "virtual" mailbox with a unique identifying name or number (called an *address*, just like a post office box). When the recipient connects to the post office, any message sent to that person is ready and waiting in his or her in-basket. As with physical mail, the recipient can open and read a message at any convenient time. On most mail systems, sending a reply is as easy as entering a simple command (or clicking once with the mouse) to create a blank message that is already addressed to the original sender. All you do is type in your reply and issue the Send command. The electronic post office system does the rest.

Unlike the worldwide postal system, which lets you drop a physical letter in a mailbox in Omaha and then delivers it to your addressee in Nairobi, electronic mail systems are not always interconnected. Many businesses support company-specific e-mail systems which can deliver messages only among corporate employees. Such e-mail systems rely on the company's internal *local area network* (LAN) to be the conduit among employees. In this case, the computer and software that is the post office resides entirely on company computers.

Another common e-mail service is run by commercial on-line services, such as CompuServe, America Online, Prodigy, and MCIMail. Users reach these services by standard phone lines. Here the concepts are the same, but the post office in each service allows all subscribers to exchange mail with each other, even if other members are scattered around the world. Some corporations prefer to use these existing e-mail services instead of establishing an internal system. This is especially useful, say, for an international company with users who may have to send mail from distant locations, where direct access to the company's central computer is difficult. A modem-equipped portable computer and an access phone number in the nearest metropolitan area are all that the user needs to reach the mail system. By accessing public commercial services, corporate users can also exchange e-mail messages with other service subscribers outside the company.

Virtually every commercial on-line service that offers electronic mail realizes that users of its service may need to exchange mail with users of other services. To that end, most on-line services provide what are called *gateways* to other e-mail services. For example, by adding the name of the MCIMail service to a recipient's MCIMail address, a CompuServe user can send an e-mail message to someone who has only MCIMail. Occasionally, closed in-house corporate e-mail systems provide one or more gateways to commercial services, allowing employees to exchange mail with customers and vendors not on the corporate system.

Perhaps the world's largest electronic postal system is the Internet. Described more fully in Chapter 4, the Internet consists of a giant global web of computers and communications links. Set up originally for government research and academic use, the Internet is currently popular with numerous corporations as well. All major commercial on-line services and many large corporate systems offer e-mail gateways to the Internet. An Internet mailbox address consists of the identifying name or number of the box, plus the name of the computing system where the mailbox is located—much like addressing a physical envelope to a box number at a particular post office building in some city. You may see people's business cards or magazine "Letters to the Editor" list an e-mail address such as this:

JoeJones@aol.com

The @ symbol (meaning "at") separates the person's mailbox identifier (to the left) from the name of the computing system (to the right). In this case, the person's mailbox identifier is a one-word version of his name (spaces are usually not allowed in e-mail addresses), and the computer is the commercial enterprise (".com") known as "aol," which stands for America Online. Some computer names to the right of the @ symbol, especially at academic and government locations, are much longer, because the mail must be routed to one of many large computers at the organization.

The lack of a single e-mail standard and addressing scheme is unfortunate, especially for e-mail newcomers. I find it bothersome when e-mailing a friend on a different system forces me to think too much about that system's addressing scheme. Fortunately most personal computer software these days shields users from the real complexities of the e-mail system on commercial services by providing address books. Addressing is a problem only for the first contact. After that the sender addresses messages by selecting the person's name from the friendly address book listing—the complex address becomes irrelevant to the sender because it is inserted automatically into the outgoing message.

E-mail messaging is an efficient communications medium, especially for people who are difficult to contact by voice telephone—and provided you're not afraid of a typewriter keyboard. Especially in business surroundings, the telephone is more of an intrusion than an aid to your work and thought flow. That's one reason high-powered executives have assistants, whose jobs include screening calls for their bosses. In truth, a lot of communication can wait. Moreover, if I'm trying to communicate an idea to someone, I'd want that person to be in a frame of mind that lets him absorb my words. Therefore, when an e-mail recipient starts opening items from the in-basket, the communication is completed on the recipient's terms—a far better prospect for the sender, in my opinion.

One reason e-mail is growing so quickly in both business and personal worlds is that it's very convenient. Sitting at your computer, you compose and send the message without having to write, print, sign, fold, stuff, address, stamp, and mail. There's also no pickup deadline at the end of the day. If you're working late, the message will still go out and be in the recipient's in-box in minutes.

Which brings us to the second primary advantage to e-mail: speed. In the communication of ideas, it's not speed that kills: it's slowness. These days it can take a week for a first-class paper letter to travel across a metropolitan area, while an e-mail message is received virtually instantaneously anywhere on the planet. No wonder frequent users of e-mail call standard postal service "snail mail."

Perhaps this particular benefit of e-mail is most obvious when communicating with someone in a different part of the world. I can send a message to an Australian in the morning and have a reply before the end of my working day, even though the other party was home in bed during part of that time. The point is that the time zones of e-mail participants are irrelevant, which is not the case with voice telephone callers. An entire electronic exchange spanning the globe takes less than twenty-four hours, without anyone getting off schedule. Here we are again, defying the ticking clock with communications technology.

We defy the clock even more with the most recent wireless two-way messaging systems tailored for mobile professionals. The devices are either small notebook-size computers or paperback-book-size communicators (also called *personal digital assistants*, or *PDA*s). The wireless data infrastructure is just now in place and working in most large cities in the United States for mobile professionals to send and retrieve data from anywhere. Sitting in an airport gate lounge, you can dial wirelessly into an e-mail service and retrieve whatever messages are waiting there. Disconnect from the service, board the plane, and read and write replies to the messages while in flight. Upon landing, tap a key or on-screen icon button to have the computer or communicator send your messages and/or faxes on their way. These wireless services are much more expensive now than connecting via the telephone wire, but in business such efficiencies are often worth the extra cost.

Electronic mail, like all electronic messaging (conferences, virtual communities, and the like), is also egalitarian. If you know (or can look up) the e-mail address of some high-muck-a-muck, you can send an e-mail message that can have the same weight as one coming from the governor. An e-mail message doesn't have engraved letterhead or fine-textured paper. A message is a message. There is a better chance that you'll get your idea to the recipient. Not only might you get a reply, but if you do, it will come more quickly than a paper letter.

If you counted all the mailbox addresses on commercial services and the Internet, you'd soon realize there are many millions of e-mail-able individuals on the planet (some addresses have even been captured and published in White Page listings). While still only used by a tiny percentage of the global population (and not all of those millions are active e-mail users), electronic mail has had a huge impact on the communication patterns and skills of many individuals and organizations.

Even in unlikely, remote, or traditionally "restricted" places, electronic mail is becoming the way to get things done and exchange ideas, both within the country and beyond. For example, during the 1991 coup attempt against Gorbachev in the Soviet Union, it was e-mail via POTS ("plain old telephone system") that kept the outside world informed of the situation from the Moscow White House, where Boris Yeltsin had encamped. These days Russian e-mail messages help independent businesspeople from all corners of the country sell and barter their wares on a network of hundreds of thousands of users. While not enjoying quite the popularity that it has in the West (personal computers are expensive, phone line quality is generally poor, and many people are still adjusting to the kind of intellectual freedom that electronic mail encourages), e-mail is playing a role in forming the new economy in Russia.

Pagers

Annoying beepers have been around for decades, but more recent technologies within the last half-dozen years have improved their ability to communicate messages to those who wear them on their belt clips or carry them in their purses.

Despite the seemingly private nature of a pager alert—a specific pager beeps or vibrates in response to a signal transmitted by the central office—the wireless technology that sends the signal is actually a broadcast. Rather than dedicate one wireless frequency or channel to each pager, a paging company usually has one or at most a few frequencies for a given geographical region (such as a metropolitan area). With a transmitter located atop a tall building, the paging company sends out message after message, intended for many pager units. All pager units hear every message, but only when the pager receives its code does it bother to capture the message and alert its attached human.

The old-fashioned paging service (still in use today) relies on a human operator, who takes a message, just like an answering service (in fact, many answering services also offer paging services). When a message for you arrives, it is written down and a signal is sent to alert your pager. All this alert does is tell you that a message is waiting for you—like the mail carrier raising the flag on a curbside mailbox. You must then telephone into the service and get the message (although we've already noted that inaccuracies may result when a human copies down the information).

A major step in automating the paging process—and sending some information along with the signal—came with pagers that included digital displays, usually just long enough to display one or two telephone numbers. When you sign up for such a service, your pager is linked to a telephone number at the pager office. If people call that number, they are supposed to use their tone keypad to enter the phone number you are to call. Unfortunately, with many of these services the user interface for callers leaves a lot to be desired; frequently there are no instructions whatsoever—

callers are supposed to know that the tones they hear are the instructions to tap a phone number. In any case, when the caller hangs up the phone, the tones are converted to their corresponding digits and broadcast over the paging radio system with your pager's code. Your pager stores the received number in electronic memory, beeps, and is ready to display the number for you. You can then telephone the person directly, without having to call the answering service.

Today, the state-of-the-art in stand-alone pocket pagers is the alphanumeric display pager. The pager unit is still a radio receiver that listens for signals addressed to it, but the page has more internal memory and a larger display. Longer text messages can be sent to the pager, often containing enough information to obviate the need for an immediate phone call back. Similar paging receivers are available as add-ons for some models of notebook computers and PDAs, such as Apple's Newton and the Tandy/Casio Zoomers. The equivalent of short e-mail messages can be sent to the device (even if the computer or PDA is turned off) and read at the recipient's leisure.

How these longer alphanumeric messages get into the paging system is an interesting combination of high and low tech. On the high-tech side, a personal computer (such as one used by an assistant in your office) can send a message from its screen to the paging service via telephone (like sending an e-mail message). But if the sender isn't at a computer or doesn't have the necessary formatting software to send such a message, it is possible to place a voice telephone call to a pager operator, who types the message into the system. It's kind of a throwback to the answering service type of paging, but until computers can reliably translate human speech into text, it may be the only way to handle a low-tech input to these kinds of devices.

The next step in pager technology is the transmission of digital voice messages that are stored in your tiny pager—like carrying an answering machine in your pocket.

In these days of pocket cellular telephones, you may wonder why anyone bothers with a pager, which separates the caller from the receiver. One reason is the cost of a page versus the cost of a cellular call. Charges for both the pagers and individual messages are getting so low that Motorola has even begun to market funky colored pagers for parents and children to use to signal each other. What was once limited to the business customer has now been extended to the general consumer. One industry research group believes that half of all new pagers have been bought for personal, not strictly business, use.

But even for businesspeople, pager technology is a step ahead of cellular telephones when it comes to tracking mobile professionals in far-flung locations. It is possible today to sign up to a pager service that will get a message to you in 90 percent of the continental United States within only a few minutes. Unlike cellular phones, pagers do not carry roaming charges or require you to register with a local carrier. The page goes out countrywide on some services, and your pager receives it no matter where you are. Some services even provide coverage in foreign countries. The ultimate goal is to have worldwide coverage via satellite. (Fortunately the satellite signals will be strong enough so you won't need a satellite dish in your vest pocket to get your page.)

Thanks to the various pager companies spread across the United States, millions of users are just a phone call away from an alert of some kind. The ability to reach someone almost instantaneously, even if just with a crude beep, is comforting not only to businesspeople (service technicians, for example, can be instantly rerouted to an emergency call), but to family members as well.

Cellular Telephones

While we're on the subject of wireless, the cellular telephone provides a good model for the power of two-way wireless messaging. The cellular phone technology we use in the United States has been available commercially only since the early 1980s. Coverage started in major metropolitan areas and now covers about 90 percent of the continental United States. The first car-trunk-mounted telephones (with handsets in the passenger compartment) cost several thousand dollars. The size and weight of phone components dropped precipitously, and phones became transportable, portable, and, today, pocketable for under five hundred dollars.

At the high initial prices, only people who depended on voice contact while on the road could make the phones and air time pay for themselves. But now that phone prices are reaching consumer price points (although air time still isn't cheap), and the phones themselves are becoming inconspicuous, the market is spreading to include family applications as well. Nearly half of such phones are now purchased for nonbusiness use. It's not uncommon to find full-time homemakers/chauffeurs on the phone while driving the kids to tennis lessons. Personal security is also a factor: family members equipped with phones feel safer while out on the streets. Admittedly, this is typically the Volvo and Land Rover brigade now, but as prices continue to lower, a personal telephone will be a common possession.

Portable cellular phones still pose some problems. Unless you turn off the phone or the ringer, it can ring inappropriately while you're in a meeting or a theater or concert hall. To prevent embarrassing ringing, many cellular phone users don't reveal their numbers and dial out only at appropriate moments to check answering machines or voice mail boxes and to return calls. This intrusive aspect of the telephone, wireless or otherwise, points toward the advantage of silent e-mail messaging systems, such as those being deployed for personal communicators, which let you set the terms of your two-way messaging.

Fax Machines

The sudden acceptance of the fax in the United States is something of a mystery. Facsimile communications—the sending of an image from one location to another—has a history virtually as old as radio. RCA began commercial transatlantic radio fax service in 1926. Some in the industry expected it to outdo nascent television as the picture transmission medium of choice for consumers when, in 1948, the Federal Communications Commission authorized fax broadcasting to consumers. The first companies to try their hand at it were a few large newspapers, including the *Miami Herald*, *Chicago Tribune*, *Philadelphia Inquirer*, and *New York Times*. Transmitting the fax signals over FM radio station frequencies that these newspaper organizations owned, publishers sought to send the daily newspaper to homes without a delivery truck. The market experiments failed, however, as television's popularity as both information and entertainment vehicle captured the visual attention of households.

On the phone lines, faxes were also being used only in limited business applications until recently. Compact and comparatively easy-to-use devices, such as Western Union's Desk-Fax, introduced in 1948, made faxing something less than the black art it had been. Still, faxing failed to catch the attention of American business until the late 1980s. Just prior to that, Federal Express thought it had found an untapped market by offering fax service between its storefront depots. While fending off aggressive competitors in the overnight delivery business, it experimented with a two-hour document delivery service, which was in many ways a fax version of the telegraph office. Not long after this idea failed miserably, businesses on their own began to adopt the fax machine as a common appliance. All the while, Asian and European business had been using desktop fax machines like telephones. Much of that usage had to do with instant exchange of import and export documents for business across trade borders—something most U.S. businesses didn't have to worry about unless they traded overseas. Moreover, in Japan and other Asian countries the documents written in complex languages (often by hand) were often best transmitted as pictures, rather than the alternative of laboriously converting them to typewritten documents.

Despite its late start, the fax machine swept the United States faster than the answering machine. Existing world standards ensured that a fax sent by a modern machine in one country would be received by a machine in another country, using a plain old telephone system line. In short order we stopped asking sheepishly if a company had a fax; today we ask straightaway for the fax number.

A received fax document takes on an air of officialdom that e-mail cannot. A fax shows stationery letterhead, a signature, and any original art that will fit through the sending machine's slit. A faxed purchase order is as good as one sent by mail—but much faster. A faxed agreement letter may not stand up in court by itself, but as a precursor to the original copy sent via snail mail, it can get the wheels of commerce moving immediately.

Faxes also seem to take priority over other matters. Despite the ease and low cost with which a fax is sent from point A to point B, the recipient usually believes a fax is urgent: "This fax just came in!" Perhaps it's the element of magic—the idea that the image coming from the machine could have been generated from halfway around the world, even though it rarely is. Still, there is that sense of immediacy about a fax. The sender sends it, the recipient's machine receives it, and the sender knows it was received—at least at the machine. Because a fax machine in an office is usually a shared asset, there is no guarantee that a fax will reach the addressee with any particular haste, but you feel good about sending it.

Perhaps one attraction of the fax machine is that sending or receiving a fax can be accomplished without a personal computer (although you can use computers for incoming and outgoing faxes, if you like). Therefore, while you could send a document as a file from one computer to another via e-mail or directly, there's no fuss about whether one computer is a PC and the other is a Macintosh—fax is its own format, and all machines can talk to each other. Computer illiterates can exchange faxes just by pressing a few telephonelike buttons.

What is perhaps most surprising is that regardless of speed, the fax is generally the lowest-quality communications medium we use today. A large percentage of fax machines in use today still require the weird thermal paper, which is impossible to write on and difficult to send back through the machine. Faxes always come in black and white, even if you are fortunate enough to use a plain- paper fax machine. Broken characters, streaks, and other illegible artifacts appear on the printout. All this, when sending a computer file between computers and printing the file on a low-cost laser printer would produce an almost typeset-quality document—it's amazing that we not only put up with fax, but adopt it readily as an essential office technology.

Be that as it may, the fax has captured a large part of business communication. It has become such a staple that even electronic mail services convert textual messages into fax images for transmission to standard fax machines. This mode is here to stay...for a while.

On-Line Information Services

Currently the domain of personal computer users, consumer-oriented on-line information services, such as Compu-Serve, America Online, Prodigy, and GEnie claimed almost 4 million subscribers by the end of 1993. Jupiter Communications Co., a market research firm specializing in on-line services, predicts that the number of subscribers will have jumped to 5.2 million by the end of 1994, a huge percentage increase. That's not taking into account the millions of Internet users worldwide.

Commercial services themselves are on the rise. In 1994 several new services started, including eWorld (Apple Computer) and AT&T PersonaLink Services. Ziff-Davis Publishing's Interchange and Microsoft's service, Microsoft Network, are scheduled to open in 1995. Each service provides e-mail (and gateways to other service e-mail systems), bulletin board communities surrounding specific interests, and collections of information that may be searched. To reach these services you need a personal computer (or personal communicator) and a telephone modem. By accessing a telephone number in many urban areas around the world, your computer gains entry to the service's central computer.

Until about five years ago the user interface to most systems was the same as it had been for a decade previous. Users were confronted with lists of sometimes cryptic choices flowing on text-only screens. Experienced users could type in shortcut commands they remembered from frequent use. Still, the atmosphere was intimidating, especially as the computers themselves began gaining graphical user interfaces, such as Microsoft Windows and the Macintosh.

To make less sophisticated users more comfortable with the services, most services have created and distribute at very low cost (or free in some cases) software that works like the other software that users are accustomed to on their graphical computers. Some services, such as America Online, were designed from the ground up to be used with such interfaces.

The most popular areas for users of these services, after e-mail, are the forums, or discussion groups, dedicated to all kinds of subjects. Since all on-line subscribers are personal computer users, it's not surprising that areas supporting IBM-style hardware and software and Macintosh computers are heavily attended. These are places where users of all experience levels read through messages left by others, bulletin board style. If a user experiences problems installing some hardware or software, or wants help in performing a certain task with a software program, it's easy enough to leave an open message to everyone in the subject forum. It rarely takes long for someone with experience or knowledge about the subject to reply. Each discussion within the forum becomes a *thread*, which users who come in later can follow from the start. It's a very democratic system; everyone with an opinion or suggestion is free to add a message to the thread.

Forums also generally have adjacent sections that contain libraries of software or other computer files that members of the forum are free to download. All the files were uploaded by other members.

A genuine sense of sharing pervades these forums. It's not unusual to get a reply to a question from an expert whose byline you've seen in a computer magazine. You also find prominent people from other walks of life who happen to share your interest in the kind of computer or software you use.

Beyond computer topics, commercial services have active forums on numerous other subjects, including hobbies and other personal interests. The point of these forums is to provide a place where people with a common interest can "gather" to exchange ideas and views and ask more experienced people for help. Groups that form around these topic areas become what have been called *virtual communities*. The "virtual" part comes from the fact that a community "gathers" around a place that exists in some distant computer. Participants are as geographically diverse as you could imagine, yet after a while frequent attendees get to know each other as friends, even though they may never see each other face-to-face.

Commercial on-line services also house electronic versions of magazines and newspapers you see on the newsstand. The value of such services to both the publishers and electronic subscribers is still being evaluated. With the combined power of a personal computer and an on-line service, it's a simple task for many users to let the computer retrieve today's stock quotes, plug the values into their portfolios, and get a daily readout of their investment values.

One blatant dissappointment among the many satisfactions of accessing these services, involves information publishing. At the moment, most services have to cater to the slowest common denominator of telephone modem access speed. To be efficient at these slow communications speeds, the information must be presented in a bland, textual manner (sometimes surrounded by fixed graphics stored on the PC). Any graphics or photographic art must be transferred to the user's computer separately and usually viewed inside a different program. When we're accustomed to looking at a magazine as visual as, say, *Road & Track*, it's jarring to see the text-only America Online version. Eventually, with faster communications speeds promised for the information superhighway's on-ramps to our doors and improved software on both the service and personal computer ends, it will be possible to present an on-screen newspaper as graphical as the printed version—more so, in fact, because the pictures could even be video clips, and page references could be "live," allowing us to click on them with the mouse pointer to zoom to that page. My fear about current on-line experiments with icons like the daily newspaper and *Time* magazine is that reader indifference may lead publishers to conclude that consumers don't want electronic versions. Perhaps demand would increase if the on-line variation provided a compelling reason to switch from the comfortable printed versions.

Cable Television

Has cable television changed our lives? For better, or worse? Cable reaches only about 60 percent of U.S. households. In other parts of the world, especially in those countries with far more government control over broadcasting, cable barely exists.

Despite the less than equal access, cable has drawn a sufficiently large audience to enable many cable television networks to stay afloat. By and large this means enough advertising revenue is generated to support the basic cable programs (USA Network, A&E, CNN, and so on) and there are enough subscribers to premium channels (HBO, Showtime, and others) to keep them going. But, as mentioned earlier, the implementation of cable is inconsistent, even where it exists. Older systems that have not been upgraded offer fewer choices than higher-channel-capacity systems installed within the last decade.

Whether a cable system gets forty or one hundred channels today, cable seems to encourage channel surfing. At the first sign of a commercial on one channel, we instinctively reach for the remote control. Some call it the "clicker." My no-tech father calls it the "gun"; advertisers would probably agree. But because the controller is there—when was the last time you purchased a multiple-viewer TV set that didn't come with one?—we use it. We use it a lot.

Cable industry dreamers equate that innate ability of viewers to shift channels with television interaction. From there these visionaries extrapolate to the conclusion that all of us watching television in our family-, living-, and bed-rooms want to interact with our video programs. This may in fact be true, but not with the stuff that's on there now. Still, channel surfing has at least gotten us in the habit of holding a wireless controller linked in some fashion to the TV set and/or VCR across the room. If the programmers should come up with compelling reasons for us to do more than hit the Channel Up or Fast Forward buttons, then we're already prepared to watch video while holding a magic wand.

If your home is cable equipped, you may have also bene-fited from your experience with the cable system. Actually, the benefit is more of a lesson—and not one the cable com-pany would like you to have learned. The lesson is your heightened awareness of the problems associated with deal-ing with a monopoly. Few communities offer choices in ca-ble companies. In general, the municipal government strikes a deal with a cable company to serve the community for a number of years before the contract comes up for renewal. Without such a commitment by local government, no cable company in its right mind would try to carve out only a por-tion of the community's business, especially considering the investment in cable office equipment and wiring to your home. But this also means that a company with old equip-ment has little incentive to upgrade frequently to offer more channels to the community. Also, if the installer fails to fix a snowy signal with any expected haste, all you can do is com-plain to the company that sets up the technician's schedule. Sure, you can get mad and disconnect the cable, but then you give up all nonbroadcast programming—some of which is actu-ally worth watching, even if you're not a WGN Cubs fan.

In the meantime we experience almost daily the results of competition for our long-distance communications business. Such competition has driven prices down and improved service dramatically. We get better-sounding conversations at lower cost than ever before. If that's what competition for the consumer dollar engenders, then it sounds like a good deal to me and would be welcome for the kind of programming that now comes down the TV cable.

Cable companies, partly because of their comfortable monopoly status, have sad customer relations histories. I was particularly curious about why regional telephone companies, which seem to have significantly improved their customer relations since their formation after 1982, despite their near monopoly would want to form superhighway alliances and mergers with cable companies. Yes, the cable companies are linked to homes in parts of the country where a regional phone company can't operate on its own, but I think phone companies would be getting themselves into a pack of trouble on the customer end by associating with cable companies. Cable companies also don't know much about programming—only about getting signals to households. All programming comes from program developers (cable broadcasters, not cable deliverers), who have a better handle on creating content.

Public statements to the contrary, I don't believe that Bell Atlantic and Southwestern Bell called off their mergers with cable giants (TCI and Cox, respectively) because of the FCC's rollback of cable rates in April 1994. My own view is that the more the phone companies uncovered details about merging such dissimilar business and technology cultures, the more they figured out it wouldn't work on a grand scale. The FCC came by with a convenient excuse that let the bigger phone company partners rationalize their potential mistakes in dollars and cents.

The changes we have experienced from exposure to cable television, then, have been unexpected and subliminal. If nothing else, cable TV has equipped us to accept controlling what we watch via a handheld remote and to encourage competition for services that will be reaching us. These are excellent foundations for adapting to many aspects of the approaching information superhighway.

CHAPTER THREE

Trails to Roads to Highways

Dusty wagon trails across the Great Plains didn't become ribbons of four-lane interstate highways overnight. Nor was the transition from one to the other the result of a single vision born in the time of the stagecoach. Instead many technologies that improved transportation speeds and convenience evolved over decades. The technologies, in turn, created demand for better roadways, and the spiral continued. Along the way, the government got involved to help fund and push along the uniform quality of major long-distance and big-city roadways, but none of the government money would have been worth much without the technology advances in vehicles and road building or consumer demand for better ways to get around.

It's clear, however, that the transition from today's data wagon trails to tomorrow's data superhighway won't take the many decades that physical roads did. A large part of the reason is that long stretches of the superhighway already exist in the unseen recesses of long-distance telephone networks and fiber-optic networks linking cable TV companies and electric utilities. That's not to say that everything the consuming public will ever need in the way of data can be handled by the current infrastructure, but at least there's a good headstart.

The final links in the superhighway system are the on-ramps that allow us, as individuals, to snatch data from the highway or send our own data onto the roads. Unfortunately, the on-ramps are the expensive and time-consuming parts of building the highway system. It means equipping many communities (or parts of communities) with new computer and telecommunications equipment at central cable and phone offices. A full implementation would also mean stringing new kinds of wires to schools, hospitals, businesses, and, eventually, our homes. And while the government is encouraging this investment in our telecommunicating future, it's not footing the bill. In fact, the government's out-of-pocket contributions will likely be limited to a few comparatively tiny research projects and, for a while, some network maintenance that consumers won't see directly. That means that private industry is responsible for completing this infrastructure.

As much as I'd like to forget about the data carriers and pay attention to the data providers, the construction phases of the superhighway's on-ramps will put the carriers very much in our faces over the next several years. This will be less the case for our superhighway access at work and school, because decisions about carriers will be made for us by the telecommunications and computer wizards at those institutions. But for personal and household on-ramps to come, those carriers will be jumping on us like used-car salespeople in loud clothes.

Drip, Drip, Drip...

Sometime in 1996 we'll probably begin reading newspaper and magazine editorials by the techno-pundits who are wondering where the information superhighway is. They'll dig (not too) deeply for the well-worn roadway metaphors about detours, potholes, road blocks, and construction zones. In a way, they'll have a right to produce those thoughts (but please hold the metaphors), because today's business news wires make it sound as though the entire highway will be in place within a couple of years and life will be nifty.

Reality check.

Regardless of the conduit of your choice (phone wire, cable, wireless), the information superhighway as envisioned by its most ardent fans will take a long time to build. Construction will also be uneven around the country.

Feeding our impatience for full deployment is the idea that the information superhighway is a single technology or technological event, like the videocassette recorder or the compact audio disc. That raises the expectations that it ships as a product, which anyone can purchase and use. Added to that expectation is the incorrect notion that the digitally converged universe will be born fully grown, or at least fully formed, as has happened with other technologies. Take the compact disc, for example. When the first CD players and CDs reached the market in the early 1980s, a technology standard had been established and agreed to by all manufacturers. Discs you may have bought to play on the first Philips CD player still play on today's CD players. Over the decade the technology has improved significantly: record producers have learned much about digital recording; playback systems have improved in their sound quality. On the consumer equipment side, home CD players, priced initially at well above a thousand dollars, can now be purchased with multidisc changers for a few hundred dollars; CD players are becoming common auto stereo installations; and you can buy a lightweight compact portable player that runs up to sixteen hours on four AA batteries. Still, when it was introduced, the compact audio disc was a stable platform, available to all.

As prices decreased and the technology improved—without sacrificing compatibility with the earliest software—adoption by the consuming public was relatively fast. Ten years later new recordings aren't even pressed as LP vinyl platters, and Tower Records is overrun with compact discs.

The information superhighway, however, is not one technology. Each carrier that comes nearest you will implement its choice of technologies at its own pace. You may hear of great advances available in the next town that you may not have available for several years, if ever. Perhaps you've heard personal computer users complain of *vaporware*—that class of computer product that is announced well before it ever ships, leaving the user in a vaporous limbo for months or years until boxes start appearing on store shelves. The information superhighway and the MIE that is to flow on it isn't just vaporware: it's *dribbleware*. Implementations of a wide range of services will appear here and there—maybe in your community, maybe not; maybe this year, maybe five years from now.

One additional faulty conception of the information superhighway as technology and product is that we know today what it will become tomorrow. That's foolish. Not only will the highway mean different things to different communities and users in those communities, but the technologies that deliver the bits and the content that those bits convey will evolve at a rapid pace. Rather than a product, the information superhighway is more of a broad concept, like audio recording. When Edison first recorded the words to "Mary Had a Little Lamb" on his wax cylinder, he couldn't possibly have envisioned today's digital audio technology and associated products like the CD player, digital audio broadcasting via satellite straight to our homes and offices, or dozens of other related applications. Electronic technologies, including personal computers, move so quickly, and are adopted by consumers in such a variety of ways, that it's nonsense to predict what will happen. It is essential, however, that we imagine what will be so we can anticipate the changes and ask for technologies that we think will help us in the future.

The Transition

Construction crews for the on-ramps will be spread out thinly, enabling some communities to get up and running much sooner than others. The early birds may not necessarily be the winners, as viewers of early cable TV systems can tell you. As the systems spread out and reach more businesses, schools, and consumers, customer demands will be better understood over time. It's likely that those farther down the implementation chain will have more fully thought out systems and services installed. Services that were either poorly designed or that offer no genuine value will be repaired or terminated. In the meantime customers may spark demand for services not yet on the drawing boards.

The next five- to ten-year stretch will be an intense period of transition of telecommunications and computer technologies. We may be on the brink of a technological change as great as the one that led the motion picture industry from silent to talking movies.

If you want to see a product of an industry in transition, beg or borrow your way to the 1929 Alfred Hitchcock film *Blackmail*. It was produced originally as a silent film. Talking picture technology was in its infancy, but Hitchcock wanted to incorporate sound into the film. To transform *Blackmail* into a talking picture, he reshot a number of scenes, recording the voices and sounds of the actors.

Watching this film offers insight into the transition we're about to experience with information. In the film, some scenes are from the silent version, with music the only sound (plus an occasional artificial effect like the slamming of a door). Other scenes have the sounds of the actors speaking their dialogue, just as in a talking picture we'd see today. While the differences in the silent and talking scenes are pretty obvious to us today (we expect full sound effects throughout), Hitchcock had one other technical glitch to take care of. The lead actress in the film, who was not a native English speaker, had too heavy an accent to be understood clearly. To cover the situation, which had obviously never occurred in a silent picture, voice was dubbed in postproduction by another actress with better pronunciation. Unlike dubbing of a foreign film, in which the actor on camera mouths one language while the dubbed voice speaks another, this was a case in which both actors were speaking in the same language. Because of the low quality of the sound (compared with later standards, anyway), the dubbing comes off flawlessly. Recording techniques at the time didn't pick up much ambient noise on the set, so a studio-recorded voice worked fine in the film.

Seeing this knitting together of old and new technologies, with the dubbing as a Band-Aid for a technical problem, demonstrates a lot about what we can expect during the information superhighway paving process for many years to come.

Who Pays?

I said earlier that construction of the on-ramps and design of the data that will go on the information superhighway will be performed by private industry instead of the government. The participating companies won't be doing it out of the goodness of their hearts. All this construction will be deemed an investment, which will have to be paid back with dividends over time. Only two sources of this payback dough exist: 1) the users of data that flows on the highway; and 2) advertisers who will try to reach the users by sponsoring data that arrives to users at no or low cost.

Straight Tolls

Setting aside the issue of "haves" versus "have-nots" until the next chapter, let's look for now at the "haves," who will supposedly be the ones paying the tolls for a lot of the information on the highway. As today's on-line computer services, cable TV companies, and video rental stores have discovered, just because somebody "has" it doesn't mean they're quick to part with it. Even if the early-adopting consumers are the higher-income households, there are still pricing ceilings for MIE services beyond which consumers won't throng. Some have suggested that $30 per month is the maximum, which may even have to include cable TV programming. Low numbers like these make potential service providers—film and video production studios, book and magazine publishers, music studios, libraries, e-mail systems—shudder.

Access to a number of these services, particularly in the messaging and information segments, will be shared by both businesses and consumers, I suspect. Venerable on-line services, such as CompuServe, found in the early days when their business was serving business that the computers and phone lines were scarcely used at night. It only made sense to offer the services to consumers at attractive prices to put those assets to use in the "off" hours. And the more the data conduits are used throughout the day and night, the greater will be the amount of revenue that can be collected to pay back the investment of building the conduits in the first place. If businesses rely on those conduits for transactions, they'll pay the prices necessary for reliability and convenience.

That may be enough to subsidize consumer use of those same assets at night and over weekends and holidays.

As the years go by, of course, the distinction between business user and home consumer will probably blur, as it often does today. Untold thousands of low-cost residential telephone lines are used for at-home businesses today. Many of these same home office professionals use computers to access on-line services for business-related electronic mail, but do so at lower rate connect times in the evening and early morning hours. Still, corporate accounts will be billed at commercial rates, while personal use (whether for business, pleasure, or both) will be billed at consumer rates. With any luck the proceeds will be high enough to allow your MIE companies to continue bringing you additional services.

Brought to You By...

Advertising, in its many forms, is another way we pay indirectly for MIE. The cost may not be out of our pockets on a monthly billing basis, but the cost of advertising a product, service, or retailer comes from the money we spend on those items or in those establishments. Just as with today's advertising, even if you don't see the ads, you pay the same price, contributing your cents or mils to the costs of ad production, space, and air time.

A valid question, however, is whether the advertising will be in the form of obnoxious billboards (test-drive Prodigy to see what this could be like) or in the form of electronic shops, where we choose to see advertisements for items we're in the mood for or want to buy.

Advertisers like to make impressions on potential buyers. What's scary about an individual's access to the information superhighway is that the highway very likely knows something about the individual as well. For example, if you are female, as described in your registration profile or as determined by a computer match of your name against a female name database, your view of the highway may contain billboards only for products that women buy. Therefore you won't be harangued by Burma-Shave ads, but "Now a word from Lady Clairol...."

Additional information about you—your demographics, buying habits, hobbies and interests—happens to be a hot commodity, which could also pave the way for advertiser subsidies of highway data you want. I'd like to think that services will ask your permission to collect this information, because advertisers might like to know, for instance, that you not only request an average of two video movies per month, but you also use the highway to place an order with Round Table Pizza each time you schedule a movie. If your information carrier collects such data (thoroughly possible in the bit-intense world of the information superhighway), it could rent that knowledge about you to the Domino's pizza place just opening in your town. After you place your order for the movie, and before you electronically saunter into Round Table, an on-screen coupon for a half-price Domino's pizza could lure you to try Domino's this time. What Domino's pays for that information about you and others in your community may help keep down the price of e-mail or local news summaries.

Ticket Takers

Interestingly enough, we are used to paying for a variety of entertainment. U.S. Commerce Department statistics reveal that consumers spent $341 billion in 1993 on entertainment and recreation, representing almost 10 percent of consumer spending (after subtracting medical out-of-pocket expenditures). Historical figures show that each year for at least the last fifteen years we devoted a little more of our available spending power to entertainment than we did the previous year. Will some of our current entertainment spending be diverted to fun served up via the information superhighway? Or will we find new forms of entertainment on the highway so enticing that we'll dig deeper into our pockets to spend even more on our total entertainment packages over the course of a year? Another question: Is it easier to spend $100 per month on a variety of entertainment events (concerts, movies, video rentals, ball games, a few magazines, basic cable TV) when the funds are distributed among many venues than to spend $50 that way and another $50 on one superhighway bill? Good questions all, but not answerable from a psychological or marketing ivory tower. Still, it is possible that a fair amount of highway-delivered entertainment will be paid for by the entertained, especially if the entertainment is something you can't get anywhere else—either because the conduit provides customized or highly interactive service or because the highway provides a time-shifting experience that makes the service worth paying for when you want it.

No matter who pays for it, however, before we can begin to welcome the highway into our lives, it's vital to distinguish the hype from the bull. Thus we now check out the myths being spread about the information superhighway and see what the realities are.

CHAPTER FOUR

The Myths—The Realities

Misconceptions about the information superhighway run rampant through the popular media. As with the local television newscaster, mentioned earlier, who made an erroneous and (for viewers) perhaps indelible link between personal computers and the information superhighway, it is incredibly easy to get bad descriptions and lunatic predictions about how the information superhighway will affect our day-to-day lives.

Fanning the flames of false promises are the commercial interests involved in the various pieces that will become the highway. When a topic such as the information superhighway becomes the hot buzzword in the media, any entity envisioning even the slightest link to it aims to position itself as a key player. To my dismay, for instance, my electronic research for this book uncovered a press release from a personal computer software company (Claris Corporation) that managed to put an information superhighway "spin" on its existing database product (FileMaker Pro), tenuous though that connection was. That's how a company tries to get visibility; start-up firms hope publicity will help them attract investment capital to turn their dreams into reality. Many companies have already made huge investments in genuine highway elements—mostly the kinds of things we won't ever see, such as high-capacity links between metropolitan areas and undersea fiber-optic links. To protect those investments they will continue to elbow their way past competitors to be in the spotlight du jour.

Every week we read and hear about new corporate alliances, megamergers that will change the highway map, megamergers that fall apart—millions and billions of high-tech dollars trading hands in the financial markets. The problem is that all of this grandstanding is within the realm of Business with a capital B. When this kind of corporate news breaks, only the business entities are involved. The engineers, programmers, and artists who create the stuff being kicked around by these business deals rarely know that the deals are taking place. While the top execs hammer out agreements in boardrooms and hotel suites, the companies are probably years away from creating something that we will actually use or see on our video screens.

It may sound as though this jockeying for attention is bad. In truth it's much better to have competitive interests vying for the dollars in our pockets than—as in the case of government ownership or monopoly by a single national provider—having no choice at all. Competitive interests in long-distance telephone service have forced its corporate participants to improve service and keep consumer costs low. The TV commercials selling these services may be a nuisance, but today's long-distance connections sound better than they ever have, and the monthly bill (at least on a cost-per-minute basis) is comfortably low.

The problem, then, is not the fact that there is and will continue to be competition in this superhighway stuff. The problem, rather, is with the hype that comes out of press releases and technology demonstrations from the competitors. It seems that the bigger the company or alliance, the more grandiose the promises. Unfortunately, the bigger the promise, the less likely it is to be fulfilled or fulfilled on schedule. I could fill a book with newspaper clippings of delayed or canceled in-the-home tests from the biggest cable and telco outfits. Also, their promises are meant to impress investors and the media—not those of us who hope to benefit from their efforts. Let's face it: at most of these announcements, there is nothing anywhere near ready to sell to us.

As a result, a number of myths have evolved about the information superhighway. These myths translate into misunderstanding about what is here today and what we can expect tomorrow. With that in mind, allow me to debunk ten of the most potentially injurious myths about the information superhighway.

Myth #1 There will be one seamless information superhighway linking all the nation's (or the world's) people.

Perhaps the most damaging notion about the superhighway metaphor is that any hookup—phone wire, fiber-optic cable, wireless signal—will put you in touch with absolutely everything that is available in digital format anywhere on the globe. In other words, an on-ramp to the highway will get you anywhere you want to go, just as it does on the interstate.

Concrete and asphalt highways are reassuring in that as long as point A and point B on a map are connected by a highway, you can probably drive your car between them, no matter how direct or circuitous the route. For the continental United States, that's very true. Get a map and plot your course. The journey may lead you across interstate highways, local expressways, freeways, and toll roads, bridges, tunnels, and even a ferry boat if necessary, but the highway will take you there.

What the paved highway analogy doesn't mention, however, is that your journey between two points may entail travel on roads built and operated under different auspices. Interstate highways are 90 percent funded by federal monies; state highways generally have a more equal share of federal and state contributions; other roads are built and maintained by counties and cities, with even smaller federal portions. As travelers on those highways, we tend not to see these distinctions. Standards for the roadway "user interface" are sufficient to make one road system not much different from any other: in the United States we all drive on the right side of the line; we know that speed limit signs are in miles per hour to match the big numbers on our vehicle's speedometer; we know that a red octagon is a STOP sign, even if we can't read. Because all roads look and feel alike, we rarely distinguish one from the other. A drive across California's San Fernando Valley from Ventura to San Bernardino (skirting the north of Los Angeles) demonstrates this characteristic of a highway system very well.

Seamless Pavements

The driving distance between Ventura and San Bernardino is 123 miles. Heading east from Ventura, you follow what appears to be a single stretch of freeway in virtually a straight line for about three-fourths of the journey, at which point you have to wake up and pay attention to the road to make a cutoff leading to another freeway. But along that first eighty-nine-mile beeline across the valley, you actually travel on three different road systems. From Ventura you begin on a U.S. highway (U.S. 101), which was part of the U.S. highway system begun in 1921 (the same system that gave us Route 66). Of course, U.S. 101, which stretches the north-south length of California, didn't start out as an eight-lane expressway. It grew to that size in places so it could accommodate the traffic in high-traffic corridors.

Continuing east, just past Studio City, you keep driving merrily while the road underneath you changes from U.S. 101 to State Route (SR) 134. You're probably oblivious of the fact, since you're continuing straight on the same Ventura Freeway you launched from back in Ventura. In a flash—and without your knowledge or permission—you've switched from the U.S. to the California road system—same multilane roadway, same signage, same speed limit, same freeway name.

Twelve miles farther down the road, you come to another of the megainterchanges you've already seen along this route. You continue straight ahead. In so doing, you change systems once more. Now you're on Interstate 210, part of the vast nationwide network designed in the depths of the Cold War. The point of the trip is to demonstrate how nicely the various highway systems across our land work together, usually transparently. You don't see the systems, how their owning agencies squabbled to gain funds to build them, how the agencies try to unload maintenance on each other—you see just the roads that take you from A to B.

It works great, doesn't it?

Well, forget about it on the information superhighway.

Data Empires

Even if you choose only one conduit reaching you or your home, the information superhighway will be far from a single system. The highway is being built by competing commercial interests. Each of these companies has a different agenda and reach. The biggest players are likely to be the regional phone companies, cable companies, and cellular phone carriers. Congress and regulatory agencies are working (slowly, some would say) to open the way for as many players to play in as many places as possible. That should encourage these firms to develop services and improve their offerings for the consumer; but it also means that what you have available to you will depend on what the service providers offer in your area.

Some services will be available on nearly all systems, no matter where you live or how you're connected. These will likely be nationally oriented services, such as satellite weather maps or forecasts on demand. In fact, it wouldn't be surprising if in return for allowing cable and phone systems to compete with full selections of "products," the federal government insists on some baseline services attached to all home access systems that would appeal to the widest audience.

Your choice of services, however, will be unique to the carrier(s) you're connected to. For example, a system based at your current cable TV company may offer a video movie library that is available in its entirety only on that system; in the next town, which may be served by a different cable company, the movie library could be smaller and quite different. The next town on the other side of yours may have its system hooked up to a database of city council meeting minutes, while yours doesn't. That's a lot like the variety of cable TV channels offered from system to system today. You'll be asking your friends whether they get such-and-such a service, just as today you may ask them whether their cable TV system has Nickelodeon so you can share a moment about last night's *Bullwinkle* rerun.

On-Line Empires

If your connection offers messaging, information, or entertainment services beyond your local service provider office, these services, too, will be different from provider to provider. A look at current on-line systems, such as Prodigy, CompuServe, and America Online, provides a hint about what this landscape will look like.

Right now, if you subscribe to any of these systems, the collection of services in their menus may overlap in functionality, but the overall content is different. For example, through CompuServe you can access the electronic edition of the *Official Airline Guide* (OAG) to look up flight schedules and a host of other travel-related services offered by OAG. This service is not available via America Online. Both systems, however, offer access to EAASY SABRE, which is American Airlines' flight schedule and reservation service. As other consumer-oriented systems become available, they will share some of the same individual services while attempting to provide unique services as well. Competition for subscribers on these PC-oriented systems is fierce, because there are only so many hours and dollars per day that personal computer users are willing to devote to these services. Competition is also fierce behind the scenes, as each system races to increase its offerings, preferably with unique and desirable services the other systems don't have.

As more systems begin actively pursuing you as a customer, they will be flaunting their exclusive services as one way to distinguish themselves from the rest of the pack. This would be like the state and federal governments competing for your long-distance travel on their highway systems by showing you that their pavements, vistas, and roadside restaurants were better than the other guy's.

As time goes by, however, content owners will probably avoid signing long-term exclusive contracts with the systems that reach consumers. There may be an initial period during which an interactive entertainment service will be distributed to homes exclusively via one of the systems, but that exclusive deal will run out. If the service is successful along the single pipeline, then other systems will sign up this service for their list of offerings. That will help the carrier(s) you connect to appear to be part of one larger system. Just as the interstate highway system reaches 90 percent of all U.S. cities with populations greater than fifty thousand, so will most on-line systems eventually grant you access to a majority of the most popular services.

Distinguishing among Empires

The need for differentiation among systems will still be great. Competition among today's long-distance big hitters—AT&T, MCI, and Sprint—offers a preview. In their case they have little to distinguish themselves in their product, because for all practical purposes a phone call is a phone call. One feature they can control is price, which is certainly an important factor for consumers. Also, as carriers were spending billions to upgrade their technologies, they appealed to us with the improved quality of the sound coming through the phone, as well as the likelihood of getting a call through quickly and with one try. Price and quality: two valid competitive factors when they can be demonstrated clearly.

Unfortunately, clarity and credibility were sorely lacking from these companies' promotions. Word of mouth became a powerful selling channel ("After switching to so-and-so, my phone bill dropped 20 percent!"). Then came the idea of encouraging word of mouth by providing special discounts to friends, family, and calling circles on the same network. This was more than just "Tell your friends." Word-of-mouth promotion was actually built into the pricing structure.

How, then, will the interactive multimedia electronic systems distinguish themselves from each other? Aside from special-interest and geographically local services, the largest differentiating force will (probably) be the virtual communities of people that gravitate to one service or another. You'll want to hang out with people who have the same interests you do. When faced with choosing a carrier, you'll end up listening more to word-of-mouth recommendations than to all the advertising in the world. It will be no different from having a friend recommend an alternate route to your favorite fishing lake because there's a better bait shop along the way.

Myth #2 You need a personal computer and must be computer literate to get onto the data superhighway.

The images we see on television news stories about the information superhighway so often show a desktop computer as the dashboard that the consumer uses to drive the highway. The primary reason personal computers seem to dominate discussions about the user end of the information superhighway is that they are readily available today to demonstrate what it's like to connect to a number of MIE services already in existence.

Computers on the Job

While the personal computer has been a hard sell to the home market over the years, businesses of all sizes have embraced it as a necessary tool to stay competitive—if you don't look for ways to improve your productivity or presentation with the technology, your competitor will, and your company will be left in the dust. Most personal computers are used at work for their stand-alone functions, which require no link to the world outside the office. A small or medium-size corporation may employ an electronic mail system for its employees, but the mail system is a closed one. No messages can come into it from outside the company, nor can employees send messages to the outside. That's not part of the information superhighway, but rather a private road behind gates that are welded shut.

Many companies of all sizes have built internal highway systems—networks—that link employees' personal computers to each other. A network that links together people within the same physical department or work group is called a *local area network* (LAN). Larger installations link multiple LANs spread around the company into one larger, *wide area network* (WAN). A WAN allows an employee in one office to send an electronic mail message to another employee in another office that may be on a different continent. Such systems may also allow users on the network to access information that is "published" on a central computer, such as the month-to-date sales of the corporation's divisions.

Users of such networks, however, don't get much of a sense of highway, because when they look at their computer screens, the network is always connected (unless there's some temporary snafu in the network) and any information located on central computers (called *servers*) appears to be in an additional filing cabinet inside your computer (even though it may be half a world away). In many ways that's good, because once your computer starts up in the morning (and you've typed your password to validate your access to the network), the network-ness of the environment recedes as you work on the messages and information that flow on your screen.

"Help! I Need Somebody..."

Unfortunately, personal computers of all kinds are too darned hard to use. At work, especially at larger companies, a department of knowledgeable folks has the job of making sure your computer and software work as they're supposed to. But you still need to know lots of gobbledygook to make sure you can locate and save information on your own computer. Graphical user interfaces, such as the one on Apple's Macintosh computers, make personal computing life somewhat easier. But even the Mac, which originally boasted about its featherlight user booklet, gets more complicated with each new operating system generation. Although not published in three-ring binders, today's Macintosh manuals still go *thunk* when you drop them on a desk.

Despite some prepackaging of computers, monitors, and software for newcomers, home personal computers are just as difficult to use as the ones knowledge workers use in the office—except at home you don't have the technical support staff to back you up. Consumers who have never used computers before are often baffled. Technical support phone lines at computer companies still get calls every week like these, reported in a *The Wall Street Journal* story:

- When the instruction on the computer monitor says "Press any key to continue," users search the keyboard in vain for a key labeled "Any."

- New buyers of laptop computers call in a panic that their computers are broken because the machines won't turn on. Prodding by the tech support person uncovers that the users expected the act of opening the lid that reveals the keyboard to turn on the computer. The users didn't look for the plainly marked "Power" switch on the keyboard.

- Another new owner of a desktop machine complained that no matter how often she steps on the foot pedal, the computer will not start. She has no idea that the mouse was something that belonged on the desktop next to the keyboard.

These computer buyers are not stupid. The computers are. Yet poor design and (what is today) unnecessary complexity drive people to feel dumb. Nearly 7 million users have sacrificed their self-esteem as far as personal computers go and have purchased books from IDG's wildly successful Dummies series, with titles such as *DOS for Dummies* and *Macs for Dummies*. It's clear that these users have come to the last resort. They *must* use the computer in their job (or have spent too much on it to stuff it away in a closet at home) and will debase themselves by lining up at the cash register holding big, bright yellow books that label them as dummies—just to make sense out of the technology. This is no way to engage new users to adopt these machines in their lives at home, away from where they are forced to use them. The truth is, the real dummies are the longtime users (count me in) who have in silence put up with quirky, fickle, and befuddling computing systems.

Computers in the Classroom

Another impression linking personal computers and the information superhighway is what is getting under way at public schools in several regions of the United States. Some of the regional telephone companies have committed themselves to bringing high-capacity fiber-optic phone lines to every public school within some states. In addition to its commitment to wire all California schools for the information superhighway, Pacific Bell has started a campaign to shuffle one million refurbished computers to the state's schools by 2000. These commitments are just for the wiring and hardware—what travels on the cable and appears on the screen is something else again. But the pilot projects that get the most publicity show students—individually and in groups—using desktop computers as the portals to information databases, videoconferences with students and teachers in other parts of the world, and other interactive learning activities involving animation and video. To get the greatest number of students and groups involved, each school needs the high-bandwidth abilities of a fiber-optic cable. It is faster and more cost-effective to establish links among high concentrations of potential users (schools and hospitals are good examples) than to string high-capacity cable or fiber to each household in the land. In other words, more people can take advantage of the information superhighway if they initially share resources, such as a high-capacity connection coming into the school or workplace.

One problem with this scenario is that except for concentrated locations, such as community centers, users at the highway hubs will be restricted to services that apply directly to the location. Companies won't let their employees call up many feature movies on demand; schools aren't going to let their students have interactive aerial dogfights with students elsewhere in the state during class hours. Choice of content will most certainly be limited in locations where your time and attention are owned by others.

Beyond the PC

While today's publicity is centered around what is possible and readily available via personal computer, work in the labs is focusing on other devices that will link us to the highway and whatever systems reach us. Two kinds of devices that will have the largest growth and most impact on our access to the highway are television set-top boxes and pocket-size communicators. Inside they may share much technology with personal computers, but on the outside they don't look or act at all like PCs.

Set-top Boxes

The first wave of set-top boxes will come to us from the cable TV companies (including wireless cable and direct broadcast satellite services). The idea of having a set-top box is not foreign to most cable TV subscribers these days. If you've been receiving all of your television from broadcast stations in your local area through a rooftop antenna, you may not be used to the idea of an extra box in the line, but the additional variety of channels often helps you adapt to the foreign experience.

The kinds of signals arriving through the cable to the set-top box will vary radically from cable system to cable system. Unlike the standard phone line, which sends a single audio signal from one source to one destination, current TV cable contains lots of signals that transmit to all subscribers' homes. At the risk of grossly oversimplifying the differences between the two, the phone company equipment does the switching that directs a signal from the caller to the receiver; the cable company sends out dozens of signals (channels) to everybody, and it is up to each user to switch to the desired signal via the set-top box.

The nature of the cable broadcast implemented on most systems today prevents individuals on the network from communicating back to the cable office via the cable. Thus, ordering a pay-per-view movie or sporting event most often requires a phone call to your cable office to alert it about your desire to watch the event. The cable company then inserts the unique ID code for your set-top box into its broadcast signal. When the event airs, the code temporarily unlocks your set-top box to allow the special event channel to pass through (or unscramble the signal). You get the feeling that the cable company is communicating directly with your set-top box, when it truth it is sending your ID code to all boxes on the system. Only your box, however, knows what to do with the code.

Some of the first "interactive" cable setups will entail the same old cable broadcast for getting programming to your home but use a telephone line to get your input back to the cable company. In light of the goal of the technology, this is as crude as using a horse to draw an automobile up a hill because the motor can't do the entire job.

Other cable systems that allow communication to go from house to cable office require only the single cable. There are a few different technologies for achieving this reverse (upstream) communication via the cable, but virtually all of them are intended for tiny amounts of data coming from any household: the press of a button on the numeric keypad of the remote control. Your communication then gets in line with others as the signal follows the cable circuit through the system, back to the cable office. There isn't the capacity to handle more substantial amounts of data, such as voice or video from a camera in your home.

What cable companies complain about today is the amount of money they must invest in their systems to upgrade for various stages of interactivity with consumers. One step is to increase the number of channels they broadcast to all those on the system. Much of this can be done with the current physical cables that come into your house, but the gear down at the cable company and the set-top boxes need new generations of technology to accommodate hundreds of channels. The phone line would still be the road back to the cable office for making selections of movies, sending back results of your on-screen menu choices (accessed via the remote control from the safety of your couch), or transmitting other information back to the office, such as your selections during an interactive game you play against another person on the network.

A more ideal—and more costly—method is to let one physical cable act like a two-way, high-capacity phone line between the cable office and you. Instead of you doing the switching between channels on the set-top box, your remote control sends a signal back down the cable to the cable company, where its computers switch your line from channel to channel for you. Essentially the cable company computer would be acting like a big, fast switchboard, hooking you up to one of the many sources of MIE that the company has links to. This is a completely different way for cable companies to think, so progress to this stage will require upgrades not only to their equipment—just about trashing their entire current office systems—but to their technological heritage.

The candidates most likely to gravitate to cable systems are entertainment services. Movies, custom scheduled television, and animated interactive entertainment lend themselves well to the lower resolutions of typical color television sets (as opposed to personal computer monitors). Moreover, feedback to the cable system via handheld remote control units isn't much more complicated than using a video game controller. There is already a consumer backlash against the complex remote controllers for today's televisions and videocassette recorders. More of the controls that now require separate buttons on the remote will be available as on-screen menus—created by user interface software built into the set-top box and updated at any time via cable by the cable company.

From Where You Sit

With all the thought and discussion about whether your personal on-ramp to the highway will originate from a personal computer or a set-top box (or both), at least one critical factor seems to have been overlooked by the engineers and marketers of these future services: where in the home we want to use a particular service and where in the home people use personal computers and set-top boxes. In fact, I believe that failing to examine this issue and underestimating its importance will cause some trial systems to fall flat regardless of their other merits. The system providers will throw up their hands and say that customers aren't ready for the technology, when in truth the technology may be misplaced in the home.

When you look at the wish lists of services that any serious player wants to produce for its customers, it would appear that the ultimate goal is to provide the fullest possible array of messaging, information, and entertainment. Regardless of the distribution method, for the immediate future all of these systems require one physical element: a visual display of some kind. For the most part, home, school, and office displays will be video monitors, ranging from standard television sets to higher-resolution computer monitors. Some of these displays will eventually be replaced by flat panel displays, similar to the color liquid-crystal displays that grace the latest laptop personal computers. The size or bulk of the display is not the issue. Rather, a video display of any kind places a huge demand on its viewer—attention.

Unlike a radio or audio compact disc, which can play in the background while we do other things, a video display insists that we literally stop and take notice. This means that devices wired into the information superhighway will be used generally at places of human rest: at a desk, near a sofa or chair, or in the bedroom. We can also stand at rest, such as in the kitchen, workshop, or garage, but the duration of our attention in those modes is short, because we're probably busy doing something else that requires our visual attention. That's not to say a kitchen wouldn't be a good spot for a video display, as long as what you need to view can be managed in short bursts, such as following along with a chef on a video that you can pause and review to keep the content in sync with your own pace (and presumably control with your voice so you don't have to take your hands out of the mixing bowl).

Equally important to the location of a video display appropriate for the home is our proximity to the display and the kinds of input devices (keyboards, remote controllers, game controllers) we use. Remember that our relationship with a display is dynamic: the closer we are to it, the more personal the experience is. One reason may be that a more detailed display, such as that on a personal computer, draws us closer to smaller elements on the screen—our focus is on a small segment of the entire screen. On the other hand, the farther away we are from the screen, the more of it we're apt to take in at a glance, and the more likely we are to accept the notion that what appears on the screen is for group showing. The larger the screen, the more inviting it is for larger groups, since everyone must sit back even farther to drink in the entire video vista. A twenty-inch TV set works well for the 2-parent, 2.1-child family group; a forty-five-inch projection TV makes you want to invite over a dozen friends for a sports event; a Sony JumboTron entertains all of Times Square on New Year's Eve.

Of the range of possible services arriving at your door courtesy of the information superhighway (at least those we can visualize today), some are personal, some are group friendly. Messaging is an example of a predominantly personal service. Text-based messaging, such as electronic mail or on-line conferences, is difficult to use in a group for a couple of reasons. One, text is more easily read from a video display that is closer to your eyes. Two, it's nearly impossible to comfortably page through long text with a group watching. Everyone reads at different speeds, so the fastest reader keeps asking the others if they're done with the current screen yet; slower readers feel dumb or embarrassed for not keeping up. Responding to or creating messages also entails typewriter keyboard entry (at least until that forever-ten-years-out voice dictation technology becomes accurate and real). Typewriter keyboards and couches don't mix well. Text-based messaging coming in via wire will work best at desktops, which are currently dominated by personal computers.

It would take some time, but video-based messaging, particularly live videoconferencing, could eventually become equally welcome at personal computer or set-top box locations. Wide consumer adoption of such services depends on the industry agreeing on a single technical standard, which would begin to increase demand for the small video cameras that could be built into set-top boxes or personal computer video monitors to capture a roomful of people for a family shot or just a lone computer user. This kind of user-to-user communication requires telephone-company-like switching (even if implemented via a cable company), rather than current cable broadcast technology.

Information is such a broad category that it will find its place in all parts of the home where a video display can get our attention. The more detailed the information, especially if it involves other work that we do on a personal computer (such as writing a school report), the more likely we'll want that information to come to us on a personal computer. But quicker-hit information, such as news, weather, and visually oriented instructional material that requires a minimum of user input, should work well in group-oriented locales throughout the home, including the kitchen and bedroom.

Interactive Entertainment

Models exist today for entertaining yourself electronically either on a personal computer or on a standard television (also on a handheld device, such as the Nintendo Game Boy). Entertainment, of course, comes in many forms. Video and movie programming, for instance, is so far predominantly passive and feels best when viewed away from the working position of a desk. Yet now there are many experiments—some of them even as shipping products—that introduce the concept of interactivity to entertainment media that have been purely passive in the past.

Voyager, a company pioneering in producing multimedia computer programs (as well as a line of laser discs of classic films that include commentary, outtakes, and other subsidiary material of interest to film lovers), ships a product on

CD-ROM for personal computers that includes the Beatles' movie *A Hard Day's Night*. Because of limitations in technology for video information playback on today's personal computers, the movie portion can be shown only in a small window on the screen. But the rest of the screen is put to use to provide additional information about the film, the music, and other elements. As viewer of the movie, you can stop and branch to any text or video in the program. This concept is clearly for inquiring minds, and it works.

Another concept whose quality and consumer popularity have yet to be fully determined is that of interactive video and movie productions that let the viewer control the story. To succeed, many varying modules of the story must be produced. As the film progresses, the user, at various junctures, is presented with plot choices—should Jessica confront Lance about the lipstick smudge on his collar, or should she let it stew within her cauldron of emotions? Depending on the viewer's choice, the next segment of the film pursues the story along lines selected by the viewer. Each time the viewer watches the film, an entirely different sequence of choices may result in different outcomes.

A startup company in San Francisco called MediaBand is extending this concept to music as well as a story line. In one of its first music videos, *Un Do Me*, the scene always starts the same, with a female club singer beginning a song (with video scene accompaniment) about an imaginary relationship with a man in the audience. At the outset, the viewer, by way of an input device that could be a computer mouse or a game controller, chooses one of four men in the audience about whom she will fantasize and sing. Depending on the man selected, the song takes wildly divergent tacks, including very different moods to the music score and lyrics. During the song, the viewer is presented with some yes-no decision points about how the singer character should react to things happening in the fantasy relationship (for example, should she jump into bed with the guy right away?). Despite what sounds like a stop-and-go way of watching a music video, the concept works: carefully written music and thoughtfully photographed video segments flow seamlessly, even if the viewer doesn't respond right away to one of the decision points.

What's unclear about this kind of interactivity is how involved viewers want to become with the art of storytelling. Do viewers simply want to see and understand the point of view of the artist who creates a song, movie, or video story? Or do they, in fact, want to influence the path a story takes, taking a different path each time they watch? Until we see enough examples of this kind of interactive storytelling, it's probably unfair to prejudge the world's reaction. But if it *should* be successful, where would we want to interact with video stories? While we may be accustomed to watching video and film in group locations, how amenable would an entire group be to taking a particular path down a story?

Personal Communicators

So far in the discussion about the computer literacy myth we've been concentrating on the world of fixed-location devices tethered to the phone, cable, or other wire-based carrier. Modern society, however, is also a mobile society. Existing wireless technology, which is rudimentary compared to the digital systems currently being installed, has already transformed life, as we saw in Chapter 2 with paging and cellular telephones. The airwaves, however, are beginning to carry more kinds of data, both to us and from us. When we leave our desks, we no longer need an extension cord to plug into the highway. Compact personal communicators (also commonly called personal digital assistants, or PDAs for short) are providing on-ramps to the highway as we move about.

Although relatively new on the market, handheld devices for personal information and communication have had a checkered past, primarily because the communication aspect has lacked the hidden data infrastructure that makes them particularly useful while on the go. Apple's MessagePad, which was built using the company's Newton technology, got off to a very rocky start, because even though it shipped in one version with a telephone modem, all you could do with it was send faxes from the MessagePad to a fax machine over the telephone. There was no software that let the device connect to any on-line service to retrieve information or exchange electronic mail. Some months later a single e-mail service became available, but the device's other shortcomings made practical use difficult, except for highly specialized custom applications.

Devices such as the Newton and other PDAs (Sharp Wizards, Casio and Tandy Zoomers, Hewlett-Packard HP-100s) begin to be useful as display devices for one-way messages sent over paging-type networks. While pagers certainly aren't new, they are often limited in the amount of information they can store and display—telephone numbers and brief messages at best. More recent technology allows longer messages to be transmitted over pager networks. A receiver not much larger than a credit card can receive and store thousands of characters of messages. You then insert the receiver into a card slot in a PDA at your leisure and read the messages fairly comfortably on large liquid-crystal displays.

Some of the latest PDA technology, such as the Motorola Envoy, go further in functionality by building in the data-only equivalent of a cellular telephone for two-way exchange of data. Like the desktop computer, such a PDA can link into a huge variety of services, including existing on-line services and services yet to be invented. Remember, a cellular connection is just a wireless extension of the phone line. Anything that can come over a standard phone line can also sail through the cellular ether.

The cost of wireless communication—the air time—is higher than the equivalent data transfer on a tethered connection. As a result, personal communicators that include wireless gear also include a jack to connect the devices to the standard phone line. If you're within reach of the phone line on-ramp, you may as well use the cheaper connection.

One supreme advantage PDAs tend to have over personal computers is ease of use. For people who don't use personal computers, the fact that PDA screens don't lend themselves well to Microsoft Windows or the Macintosh user interface is a blessing. Instead, PDA designers have had a chance to redefine the state of the art of user interfaces, providing users with interfaces that make sense for riding the information superhighway. The Magic Cap interface, developed by General Magic, for example, was designed from scratch as a consumer-friendly user interface for personal communicators. Motorola has adopted Magic Cap for the Envoy communicator, as has Sony for its Magic Link wired communicator. Other name brand products will also be built around this interface.

Partly as a way to cover the high costs of early personal communicators, and partly as a way to get early customer feedback about desirable features, many manufacturers aren't throwing every bell and whistle into today's devices. Instead they're designing tightly focused products. Moreover, the wireless information infrastructure is also still under construction, so the PDAs can deliver only what the systems allow. In one sense the trend toward a range of special-purpose wireless devices is disturbing. At some of the conferences I attend (admittedly frequented by the more technologically pliable individual), it's not unusual to see attendees with a pager clipped to a belt and a cellular telephone tucked away in a pocket or purse. On top of these gizmos, connectivity-conscious people will probably add a wireless data PDA to their kit bags. I hope the trend moves toward developing single compact devices that cover a multitude of communications and information tasks. There's no reason (other than cost, for the moment) that pager and voice mail services couldn't be built into a pocket cellular telephone. Or that a voice cellular phone couldn't be built into a data communicator—especially since the same cellular telephone wireless network would probably work for both types of communication (Bell South's Simon communicator is a first attempt at such a device). I really want to avoid having to carry a chain of PDAs in my briefcase with as many special-purpose devices on it as I have keys on a key chain. A PDA chain will not be convenient, fun, or cool.

For the computerphobe, the good news is that with the proliferation of advanced set-top boxes and PDAs, computer literacy won't be a prerequisite for accessing the information superhighway.

Myth #3 The Internet is the superhighway.

You can't have read much about the information superhighway without hearing about something called the *Internet*. As I write this, bookstores are selling more titles about the Internet than about Microsoft Windows—and have been for several months.

What I find strange about all this hoopla is that the Internet is one of the most difficult-to-use, anarchic on-line worlds you could imagine. Ordinary consumers with personal computers can't just call up a place called the Internet Company, supply a credit card number, and become a subscriber or venturer on the Internet. Access is possible by connecting a personal computer to a larger computer, which acts as the Internet provider and *node* on the network. Your connection may be through a dedicated data phone line, a corporate or university data network wire, or, for some Internet providers, a plain telephone dial-up line. You then use the node's computer and its Internet software to connect with other nodes around the world, linked together with high-bandwidth data lines.

The Internet Defined—Sort Of

The Internet is unique, to say the least. It's not a service per se, like CompuServe or Prodigy. It is actually an inter-linked network of hundreds of thousands of computers located at government, education, and corporate sites around the world (although the bulk of them are in the United States). Despite its complexity, unfriendliness, and restricted access, the Internet is said to have millions of users. No one knows for sure how many people surf the Internet. Since there is no central membership body, there are no subscription lists. Instead researchers have tried using statistical methods to estimate the population. Guesses range between three and thirty million—quite a gap. We may never have an accurate count.

Like a lot of infrastructure technology, the Internet began in the 1960s as a comparatively primitive network of computers whose users were performing various types of military and government scientific research. Some of that research, sponsored by the U.S. Department of Defense, had to do with the network itself. Experts knew that in the event of an enemy attack, part of a government communications network could be wiped out with a well-targeted nuclear device. The idea was not only to distribute libraries of information in multiple computers located in a variety of physical locations, but also to establish linking facilities that would allow a message to go from computer A to computer B through any of the surviving links and computers on the network. In other words, rather than one outage crippling the entire network, a damaged computer would just become a dead spur, while all traffic would be routed automatically along the remaining paths. Very clever.

In the process of building these computing centers and networks—all with government funds—more scientists at the linked institutions uncovered the value of instant communication with others in the same field. Not only could colleagues in different locations work together fairly efficiently (and for free), but findings could be published immediately to their academic communities, long before an article could be accepted and printed in a scholarly publication.

Of course, people being people, the all-work-and-no-play aspect of computer networking wore thin. After a little bit of initial alarm by the funds dispensers, special-interest sections began planting themselves on various computers within the Internet. Here, users with similar interests could post messages on any topic or opinion that was covered by the subject. The computer might also contain some computer file archives (text or pictures for reading on personal computers) of interest to everyone in the group. The network software intended originally for exchanging research and work-related files was soon forwarding files of data from these libraries to any individual on the network. Not surprisingly, the first group set up by the wireheads who spent the most time on the Internet was one specializing in science fiction discussions. But pretty soon groups of all kinds started populating the Internet.

Where the Action Is

In addition to electronic mail, the Internet provides bulletin-board-like places, called *newsgroups*, where users can hang out with others around the world with the same interests. All of these newsgroups (together called UseNet) adhere to the same communication *protocols*, so that they respond to the same set of commands for reading message threads, adding a message to a thread, and so on. The computer that acts as your service provider runs news reader software that helps you locate and manage the newsgroups you check into regularly and their messages.

With roughly five thousand different newsgroups of interest to the public, it may take you a while to locate all the newsgroups that mesh with your personal interests. And those interests range far and wide, from cultures in specific countries to classical music to the television cult series *Mystery Science Theater 3000* (MST3K). Anyone can join in to read, ask questions, engage in debates, or help others within the subject area.

The other prevalent feature of the Net (as the entirety of all computers that can connect to the Internet is called) is information—specifically, the vast public libraries of information stored on various university, government, and corporate computers worldwide. Some of the data is serious (such as the U.S. Census Bureau analyses), some is frivolous (episode summaries of *The Simpsons*). Using Internet software tools that reside on your service provider's large computer, you can copy files to your own computer. The files may be informational, pictorial, or for your computer (such as sounds or public domain software). Some of the terms you'll see to access other computers are commands you enter to start the process (gopher, telnet, or ftp, for file transfer protocol). Having helpful user interface software can soften the complexity somewhat, but there is no centralized directory of what's available on the Internet.

Whether you work with graphical interfaces or the old-fashioned Unix commands of your service provider's computer, it's easy to blow dozens of hours looking through file directories and messages (Net surfing) for information pertaining to the interests of your choice. The sense of place, which is mostly on distant computers but also partly in the mind of the user, is known as *cyberspace* (coined in William Gibson's 1984 sci-fi classic *Neuromancer*), and navigating cyberspace is a passion for many.

Only as recently as 1988 did the Internet begin to grow so massively in its capacity and reach. Between 1988 and 1992 the number of host computers on the Internet grew from approximately thirty thousand to over seven hundred thousand. Today Vice President Gore continues to look to the Internet as a model for the information superhighway. That's what leads many people to think that the Internet and the information superhighway are synonymous.

Under Siege

But linking the restricted world of the Internet to the theoretically public world of the information superhighway is a dangerous practice. For one thing, the Internet is not only experiencing growing pains under the pressure of tons of new users each year, but its very nature is undergoing a transformation. Internet old-timers are used to free access, with the government picking up the tab through the National Science Foundation (NSF), the U.S. Department of Defense's Advanced Research Projects Agency (ARPA), and other grants. However, while the government gladly supports advances in high-speed telecommunications networks and supercomputer centers as ways of staying globally competitive in the technology race, it isn't interested in setting up credit card billing for your children's forays into the virtual Library of Congress and downloading full texts of books for a term paper.

That brings up another sea change that has upset old-timers: commercialization. While the keepers of the Internet ethic tend to be members of a high-tech priesthood, they are nevertheless very egalitarian among themselves. Information published on the Internet has traditionally been free to all comers. This naturally clashes with longtime capitalist *newbies* (newcomers) dressed in Internet clothing who view the Net as a distribution and advertising medium for commercial wares.

Thus a battle is brewing between the visionaries who set up the Internet in the first place and those who want its services to be self-sustaining or profit-oriented. Longtime users who have roamed Internet cyberspace for hours every day without spending a dime from their own pockets will resist the implementation of toll booths or taxi meters on this part of the information superhighway. Responsibility for development and maintenance of certain parts of the Internet is being handed over to commercial concerns, including heavy hitters such as Sprint, Ameritech, and Pacific Bell. This *really* scares the Net-heads.

Commercial interests are making headway, however, in using the Internet for advertising. An environment called the World Wide Web (WWW) allows anyone to publish screen pages of text and graphics, which Internet users (who have appropriate viewing software) can then access and browse through at their leisure. By avoiding existing Internet sanctuaries, WWW providers have discovered how to publish information in a way that doesn't intrude on existing cultures.

Despite all this transitional turmoil, which may go on for several years, there is a wealth of information and thousands of communities of informed people tucked away on these hundreds of thousands of computers. Assuming you can gain access through an academic institution, your place of work, or the few pay-as-you-go gateways for individuals currently available (the WELL in the San Francisco area, the national service DELPHI, and NetCom On-Line Communication Services in San Jose, California, are three examples), finding your way around is a trick in itself. Many of the pages in the

Internet books I mentioned earlier are devoted to directories of special-interest areas. There seems to be at least one discussion or news area for every hobby, lifestyle, family, medical, career, and professional interest under the sun—far more than you can find on the largest consumer services such as CompuServe or Prodigy.

Commercial services caught up in the Internet fever are now working relentlessly to provide easier access to the Internet. At most they can make navigating the Internet friendly, by letting users click on icons or text lists with mouse pointers in Windows or Macintosh front-end software. As I write this, America Online and CompuServe have come furthest along, providing their graphical user interfaces to access UseNet and gopher services on the Internet.

Regardless of the interface, friendliness ends at the screen. Once connected to the Internet world, users are on their own to interact with the other users (and hard-core Internet users regard the graphical interface users of America Online and CompuServe as wusses, cascading over the wall to clutter up the Net). As in any community, there are nice people and there are wackos. In the on-line world, people who might ordinarily be shy can lash out at unsuspecting users—primarily in the delayed messaging of the bulletin-board-like service. Such key lashings are called *flames*, and it's pretty hard to be active in a group for long without someone flaming at something you "say" in the group. You may also find flamers who expend great energy parsing your grammar and logic while you try to get an idea across to the group or debate a point. When I get involved in these kinds of exchanges, I generally let a flamer have the last word while I move on to something else less irritating. Not everyone can do that—a flamer can really get your dander up—but I prefer not to get mired in such time-wasting communications.

The Great E-Mail Gateway

Whether or not you use the Internet directly, it's likely that as a commercial service user you have employed the Internet as an intermediary for an e-mail message or two that originated in another service. The popularity of the Internet has forced virtually every commercial service to provide e-mail gateways to the Internet. At the same time, each of these services is set up as a host on the Internet to receive mail for its users. As long as the message's address includes the Internet name of the host computer (such as @compuserve.com), there's a good chance the message will reach your friendly in-box.

Receiving a message that came via the Internet is a scary event the first time. First of all, some services charge extra for using the gateway, even for messages that come to you without your knowledge. But the real surprise comes when you open the message. Even a one-line "howdy-do" turns into a monster message that includes a dozen lines of terrifying codes, addresses, numbers, and other gobbledygook. Unfortunately this is the baggage an Internet e-mail message must carry with it to arrive at its proper destination, regardless of routing, and to assist a reply to find its way back to the message's originator. For the most part you can ignore all the hieroglyphics, because when you reply, your commercial service software handles the addressing.

By virtue of its high-speed data transfer characteristics and its ubiquity, the Internet has become a common highway for otherwise incompatible e-mail systems. Many corporations link their own internal e-mail systems to the Internet so the companies can communicate via e-mail to customers and vendors on the outside.

Yet for all its content, depth, and omnipresence, the Internet will likely play only a subsidiary role in the information superhighway. If Internet special-interest communities get too popular, the feeling of community in those "places" will diminish, just as a small town that grows into a city loses its original flavor and charm. The Internet, then, will become one of the highway systems that will make up the great information superhighway. It may have more access points than most, but a lot of work is still needed to develop software that will make the scary Internet world a warm and fuzzy place to browse. Another growing problem (covered in more detail in Chapter 6) is that the uncontrolled nature of the Internet makes it more vulnerable to hijinks by pranksters. This could threaten the credibility of the virtual community asset of the Internet that, today, is one of its strengths. In the long run, everyday on-line users may prefer a more closely moderated cyberspace to protect themselves from being scammed.

When the industry hears Vice President Gore citing the Internet as a model of the information superhighway, I believe they're receiving the wrong message. The part to be modeled is the communication infrastructure that links the computers behind the scenes. More visible aspects of the Internet, particularly the cultures that have grown within, do not welcome the technically unwashed. Better models exist for the human connection, while the Internet may be seen as the glue transparently uniting the on-line world, working much as the long-distance telephone network does for consumer calling.

Myth #4 CompuServe, Prodigy, America Online…are the superhighway.

This myth is highly analogous to Myth #3 about the Internet. It all has to do with your frame of reference. To an Internet-savvy individual, commercial services are like kiddie toys, where Aunt Bea can exchange recipes or Joe Newuser can ask about the differences between the Diskcopy and Copy commands from DOS. It must be what Harley bikers think of Vespa owners. Those services are such sissy places, where you can see complete menus of available services and navigate by clicking on-screen buttons with a mouse, Net-heads must think.

Be that as it may, if the information superhighway is to appeal to the general public, it had better have a friendly user interface and provide easy mental models for its users. The latest graphical user interfaces for commercial services are headed in the right direction, hiding what used to be very intimidating screen prompts for commands to be typed from the keyboard.

Many to Choose From

There is, however, a scary side to the commercial services: their proliferation. Sure, competition is good, but when users have to choose among a dozen or more services to dial into from their personal computers or PDAs, the on-line world becomes less appealing than today's highway planners might hope for. As of this writing, the most popular commercial on-line services are as follows:

America Online
AppleLink
CompuServe
DELPHI
GEnie
Prodigy

New services launched in 1994 include the following:

AT&T PersonaLink Services
eWorld (Apple Computer)
Interchange (Ziff-Davis)

Then there are the more prominent dedicated commercial e-mail services:

> MCIMail
> NewtonMail (for Apple's Newton)
> Radio Mail (wireless service)

Each is just one existing system on the information super-highway, with many more to come (Microsoft is at work on its own system, called Microsoft Network). With potentially tens of millions of users outside those who are on the Internet alone, there will be plenty to go around, but the diversity of services will have other effects on the highway.

One-to-one messaging—e-mail—won't be much of a problem, because if you subscribe to any one of these systems, you have a mailbox that can be reached from any other system, primarily through an Internet gateway. Some e-mail user interfaces are easier than others. For example, to send a document file and a descriptive note from one user to another on CompuServe, you must send two separate e-mail vessels: one for the file and one for the descriptive note. More common, however, is the method of sending a file that has a descriptive note attached to it. Together they appear as a single e-mail message in your in-box. Whichever method you prefer, it is unlikely that you will choose a commercial service based on its e-mail capabilities. The same functionality exists on practically all systems.

Distinct Communities

Messaging of the bulletin board variety, however, is quite another subject. Special-interest bulletin boards are the communities to which you choose to belong and contribute. The members are the people you hang out with. The libraries associated with those forums are where you can obtain member-supplied treatises, reviews, software—all kinds of things related to the discussion area. If you belong to one service, you may not be aware of how your favorite discussion areas are populated on the other services. It's possible that your hobby isn't well supported or popular on your service, while on another service it's one of the hottest subjects around. Unless you hear by word of mouth which service has the best forum for your areas of interest, you may never know what you're missing.

I see the disparity from service to service all the time. Each day I regularly check into three commercial on-line services plus the Internet. All four worlds have sections covering computer interests of mine, but they are not connected to each other (except for mail). Occasionally I'll see messages left by the same people I've met on multiple services, but by and large users tend to become faithful to a single service. Typical users don't want to pay for more than one service. Specific discussions on each service vary widely. Some issues that are real hot buttons on one service don't even appear on the others. Many services offer similar libraries of software and other documents, but there are definitely items in one library that never appear in the others, even though they would be valuable to all.

For one of my hobbies, there are forums in two commercial services and a few related newsgroups on the Internet. It became clear after only a few days of *lurking* in these forums (reading the messages without contributing any answers or comments) that the amount of traffic on one of the services was several times that of the other services. Moreover, the individuals on the more active forum were generally a literate, well-informed group, eager to help with any problems other members had. If I had belonged only to the less populated service, I would have rarely checked into the hobby forum, because it was dull and nearly empty. I would have never heard about the great times had over in the other services.

I suppose this is no different from belonging to a local photography club, where you get to know the members and your meeting discussions and presentations are based on what the members find interesting. However, with this type of group, breadth of membership is bounded by geographical limitations. An on-line community knows no geographical boundaries; the only boundary is that of membership.

I wonder, however, if the expectations are that a wide geographical pull means the widest pull of ideas and expertise. If so, then the Balkanization of on-line service forums could create electronic turf wars of a sort. The coin collecting group on Prodigy may believe it is *the* place for coin collectors: to belong to the coin collecting forum on another service means nothing.

Will membership in a particular on-line service forum be cause for a quasi-religious battle of the forums? Consider two friendly neighbors who share the same interest in growing tomato plants. Each belongs to a gardening forum on a different service. Despite their physical proximity to each other, each friend has an entirely distinct set of on-line friends who also know a thing or two about growing tomato plants. One forum may have a good library of tomato plant food recipes, while the other has active and instructive discussions about pest control. The two members start as friends but end up traveling in different cyberspace circles. To me this carries the same awkward feeling I had as a kid when my best friend's parents sent him to a different school. While we two friends shared many interests and good times together, each of us had entirely different worlds of people and experiences that the other never fully knew or understood.

Unfortunately, the more services there are that carry the same special-interest forums, the more distributed will be the on-line world's base of knowledgeable people in those

areas. Two great minds may never meet. The opposite scenario—one giant service—would also have its share of problems: if a discussion area gets too big, the same two minds
may still never meet. You can see the problem already in
some Internet newsgroups, where two hundred new messages can appear in less than twenty-four hours.

The Uniqueness Challenge

Information publishing on commercial services will also exhibit the Balkanization of forums. As described earlier, each
service will strive to publish information that the others
don't have in order to differentiate itself from the other services. I believe exclusive electronic distribution through one
service would be suicidal for some information publishers,
unless the exclusive arrangement is for a limited time and is
used as a test bed to work out the kinks in the system. Take
the experiments going on today with various daily newspapers that are linking up with individual services. The *San Jose
Mercury News*, for example, is available through America On-
line; the *Atlanta Constitution* can be read daily via Prodigy.
Were I the publisher of a daily newspaper, I would consider
it foolish to limit the electronic market to subscribers of only
one on-line service. Today only a small percentage of local
readers are on-line with *any* service, so of course an even
smaller percentage are on-line through a *particular* service.
And the chance that a daily newspaper will attract significant steady readership outside its primary geographical market is pie-in-the-sky thinking. *USA Today* or another national
newspaper (including *The New York Times*) might get away
with it, but not metro-specific papers.

Still, as the commercial on-line services seek to provide
exclusive services, no one of them will probably offer everything you'd like to access every day of the year. No matter
how well you plan it, the service(s) you subscribe to will lack

access to some information base you'll want to search for pleasure, school, or work. The fact that the highway is not one contiguous system will get in your face the hard way. The best you can hope for is that the service you choose will have a gateway to the Internet and what you need can be found there—provided you can wade through the Internet's vast archives.

Myth #5 Interactive multimedia is the information superhighway.

Because I was active in early Macintosh software that popularized the concepts of multimedia—a software tool called HyperCard—I am ultrasensitive to the abuse that the word *multimedia* gets. A purist could say that multimedia is an electronic presentation consisting of two or more of the following media:

Static Media	*Time-Based Media*
Text	Sound
Graphics	Animation
	Video

I would define the term to include two or more of these media provided there is at least one representative each from the static and time-based columns. Of course, that means that a lot of what's on television is multimedia, including the screen showing a Ginzu knife in action, next to a toll-free hot line for ordering.

That's why good multimedia, whether or not it says so in its description, must be *interactive*. Interactivity is another vague and misused concept. Some would call the Ginzu knife commercial interactive multimedia, because you can change the channel or lower the sound with the remote control. Sorry, but I draw the line there. The goal of interactive multimedia should be to *engage* me, not turn me off. If the commercial and television allowed me to place an order for a set of knives via my remote controller, then I'd finally agree that the experience qualifies as interactive multimedia.

Prehighway Multimedia

Because we don't have the conduits in place to deliver true interactive multimedia products to our TV or computer screens live, the publishing medium of choice these days is the digital disc in either the compact disc-read-only memory (CD-ROM) or compact disc–interactive (CD-I) format. With so much multimedia product being shipped in these formats, some commentators equate such discs with interactive multimedia. The fact is, digital data discs might contains hundreds of megabytes of dull, silent text or a library of static art. By one count, 80 percent of all CD-ROM titles are high-priced, business-oriented databases of valuable but incredibly boring facts and figures. Therefore don't confuse CD-ROM or CD-I with interactive multimedia. Look instead to the content on a disc before categorizing it.

The industry has also gotten into trouble bandying about the "m" word by rushing out with too many products of questionable quality under the multimedia banner. Occasionally a good product comes along, thoughtfully combining perhaps four or five different media as well as intelligently designed interactivity. I feel this way about the *Animals!* CD-ROM produced in part by the San Diego Zoo. While not exactly presenting the San Diego Zoo in electronic fashion (which would be a wonderful extension to the disc), this program nevertheless allows users to wander among the disc's collection of animals in a variety of ways—at random, by climatic zones of the animals' native habitats, and so on. At screens depicting most animals, you can click an on-screen button to hear the sound that the animal makes or view video clips of the animal in live action. You can even take different slices of the information on the disc by selecting from a list of all the videos or all the sounds.

The *Animals!* disc was intended for children, but even as an 80 percent adult who had become disenchanted with CD-ROM products, I was thoroughly engaged while traveling through this virtual zoo. My first reaction was that I wished I had other discs in the same format that would teach me about other things, such as astronomy or architecture. Working with this disc also renewed my faith in the promise of interactive multimedia, regardless of the delivery conduit.

As demonstrated in this primarily educational example, multimedia can add value to the information part of MIE. Multiple media have also been a part of video-game-like entertainment for more than a decade (does anyone else remember the Atari 2600, Intellivision, or Coleco video game systems?). Interactive entertainment, however, isn't what it used to be. With entertainment hardware capable of displaying real-time video on the screen (usually stored on a CD-ROM, as in the 3DO game system), animation by itself may not be good enough, unless the quality is extremely high.

Blending Video with Other Media

Most of the video that rides atop animation in today's state-of-the-art entertainment titles reminds me way too much of the Hitchcock movie, mentioned earlier, which grafted talking scenes onto an originally silent film. In most of the available titles I've seen, the two motion technologies are not well integrated. Sometimes the video is a gratuitous clip that appears in a separate window on the screen (such as a real NFL referee signaling a touchdown after a completely animated football team has scored). Other times the video lies atop cartoon animation, but not with the subtlety you see in the film *Who Framed Roger Rabbit?* When the two media don't mix well, the viewer is too aware of the graft. The minute you begin seeing more of the technique than the content, the spirit is lost.

Contrasted with this is the First Person series of CD-ROM products from Voyager. Each title in the series starts with an electronic version of a printed book. The first title is Marvin Minsky's *The Society of Mind*. The plain text content is enlivened by the author, who, at the reader's request, appears as a video character to amplify a point in the current screen of text or graphics. Through some clever video photography, the author appears to walk around graphical images on the screen "page." If you want to witness an effective early effort at making a page of a book come alive, this series is something to behold.

Interactive Shopping

Another CD-ROM that shows how we could use interactive multimedia on the information superhighway is an electronic catalog produced by Apple Computer. Called *En Passant*, the disc offers an eclectic collection of products from well-known mail-order brands, such as L. L. Bean, Williams-Sonoma, and the Nature Company. Working with the computer that is required to access the catalog, the disc's software lets you browse through the products by catalog brand name (as you would if you received the catalogs in the mail) or by product category. For example, if you want to select a business gift, the software presents a selection of products that fit that category from a variety of catalogs. Organizing the products of a dozen catalogs by product type is impossible with the paper versions, so the CD-ROM offers both traditional and innovative ways of shopping via catalog.

Some of the catalogs on disc offer an engaging application of interactivity: how you can view clothing available in multiple colors. On the screen for, say, a sweater, you see a typical four-color catalog photograph with a model wearing the sweater. Also on the screen are small swatch squares that show all the colors the sweater comes in. By clicking on each color square, the sweater on the model changes to that color. Seeing the whole sweater in the color of your choice is significantly better than trying to visualize how it will look from a tiny swatch.

As good as this first attempt at electronic shopping is, the disc misses an important part of automating the experience to magic levels. Once you have assembled an order from your products choices, you must use the telephone to call in and place that order by voice. Perhaps the designers of this shopping disc wanted to crawl before walking, but the next logical step is to have the computer place the order with the central order takers via modem or fax. Admittedly not every computer has a data or fax modem, so perhaps the CD-ROM program designers also felt that the feature wouldn't be used by enough electronic catalog browsers to be worth the effort. To my way of thinking, this extra feature would have closed the loop on an otherwise well-executed experiment.

From CD-ROM to High-Bandwidth Conduit

The work being done today by software and traditional publishers for distribution on CD-ROM is a good training ground for when the conduits to our homes are wide enough to ship the same kind of information along the information superhighway. To justify their success, multimedia presentations must consist of information or learning that users consider valuable. Also, user interfaces must be desirable to be successful. However, publishers shouldn't put 100 percent faith in their CD-ROM user interfaces as those that will be welcomed in on-line offerings. For one thing, people using most CD-ROMs are personal computer users. To get the CD-ROM to run, they've already mastered a complex interface such as Windows or the Macintosh. Yes, these interfaces are far easier than DOS or Unix, but they're not the kinds of interfaces most home users will want to see on their family room television sets.

Good multimedia composed of text, digital audio, and digital video requires a large quantity of bits to reach the user's gear every second. Even with today's best commercially available compression techniques, you cannot get top-quality, real-time multimedia through a plain old telephone system phone line. Cable would do a better job in the near term, but the interactivity will either be limited (through the cable) or cumbersome (through a phone line). And to convey high-quality interactive multimedia via the wireless airwaves requires communications systems distinct from the current cellular systems. I can safely say that the best multimedia will be delivered predominantly on media such as CD-ROM for some time to come. While interactive multimedia has the potential to engage a huge audience, the information superhighway on-ramps will require the much higher-capacity conduit per household to handle the bits, even for something as comparatively simple as home shopping.

Myth #6 Only the "haves" will be able to afford the tolls on the information superhighway.

The fact that the information superhighway has become a part of public policy—even if the policy dictates that private enterprise is responsible for building the rest of the highway—has forced critics and boosters alike to address the issue of equal access. With today's information wagon trails, those who can afford personal computers, on-line service charges, fancy cable systems, and personal communicators are the ones with the access. The concern is that only the wealthy will have access to the MIE on the information superhighway.

Assessing Needs

Questioning the right of access for a wide range of family economies assumes there will be something on the highway that everyone needs. *Needs*, not *wants*. Obviously I'm not talking about basic human needs of food, shelter, and clothing, but rather the information or connectivity that people need to be part of the current society or their communities. What those information and connectivity needs are varies around the world. For example, in the United States a household telephone is considered enough of a need for the government to require that low-cost "lifeline" service be available to low-income households. Such folks don't need fancy calling plans or call-waiting, but our culture has grown around the telephone infrastructure, so it can be said in all good conscience that Americans need at least the ability to dial 911 in an emergency or receive a call from a neighbor or family member. The situation is quite different in China. Ordinary Chinese families have only recently been allowed to apply to have telephones installed in their homes. Almost one million people are on a waiting list to spend one to two years' wages for the privilege of having a line installed. More than half of the rural villages have no phone service whatsoever. Chinese culture is not built around the telephone, so the common citizen perceives little need for such a service.

At the moment, the average American must perceive the information superhighway with the same distance and skepticism with which the average Chinese views the plain old telephone. With the possible exception of messaging, there is little in the way of electronically distributable information and services that most people need day to day that isn't already available nearly for free. Even the near-term promises of video on demand, particularly as it applies to electronic equivalents of movie video rentals, adds little value beyond the convenience of not having to visit the video rental store. I have yet to hear of compelling information and entertainment that would fall under the need category, even for the "haves," much less the "have-nots." I'm confident such services will evolve, however, which is why it's important to be aware of the access issue.

Access is such a front-burner topic for architects of the information superhighway that I believe it will be addressed on the economic front at least as well as it has been for to-day's utilities: energy, telephone, and cable television where broadcast TV reception is not possible. Whether imposed by the government or presented as a goodwill gesture by the highway's builders and toll takers, universal access for basic services (whatever they may become) is assured. The cost will be borne, as it is for the other utilities, by business cus-tomers and, to a lesser extent, by customers who can afford the regular fees.

The Literacy Barrier

Economic status, however, is only one divider between "have" and "have-not." Even if the most compelling applica-tions should become available at no or low cost tomorrow, there would still be a significant division between the literate and illiterate members of our society. These groups, in my opinion, are the true "haves" and "have-nots" on the infor-mation superhighway. If a person can't read text that comes down the off-ramp, then it's not text or information: it's vis-ual noise. Some might argue that the pure implementation of the data highway won't involve text at all—every piece of messaging, information, and entertainment will be motion video and/or sound. Even if that were true, the technology, infrastructure, and content that could make that textless world possible are decades away. In the meantime there will be many individuals of all ages in every country of the world who won't be able to understand what text there is—and there will be plenty of text for some time to come.

As scary as this may sound, the information superhighway can instead play a role in reducing the number of literacy have-nots. Some lanes of the information superhighway *must* be reserved for teaching reading and writing skills to both children and adults. Let the courses cycle over and over for years on a basic cable channel service—even subsidized by advertising if the government won't kick in some dough. As the best in interactive multimedia, this would be a stimulating early offering to course its way down the information superhighway into as many homes as possible.

Access to Government

While I'm on the subject of access, I express concern over government policy interest groups who view the primary purpose of the information superhighway as giving every citizen access to the bowels of government. The false assumption here is that most Americans care enough to track legislation, express an opinion to a Washington politician, or read a transcript of a presidential proclamation. Despite (or because of) instantaneous news coverage and the relative ease of eavesdropping on Washington's daily business via the C-SPAN cable network, voter apathy is at its highest level, as is overall distrust of politicians and politics. It's clear that at the moment, the general public does not share the enthusiasm of public interest groups participating in high-tech policy-making in Washington.

Public participation in Washington politics may even be impractical. How can congressional staffs keep up with a huge influx of electronic mail without merely sending back e-mail form messages? If senders don't believe their messages are being read, they'll eventually stop sending—tuning out even further. The builders of a representative democracy didn't foresee instant access to the government by every citizen. Or perhaps they did, which is why our democracy is representative rather than direct.

Despite my pessimism on this front, I believe there is a place for citizens to be involved via the information superhighway, even if the road merely circles the town. On the local level it is possible to manage the input from concerned citizens in municipal affairs. Fremont, California, for example, has set up a computerized bulletin board service at its Chamber of Commerce. Citizens can obtain minutes of city council meetings and other information about local events. Such interaction with a local community's government is an appealing application of this technology. As in Deerfield, Illinois, where home cable TV viewers of village government meetings can telephone in questions, so too could broader two-way communications systems invite this level of participation. Wouldn't it be convenient to look up zoning regulations, apply for permits, and get e-mail responses to questions from your community government? With computer terminals available to all at City Hall, the local library, and even coffee shops, the economic haves and have-nots could gain equal access to local government. Local business sponsors could get programs like this off the ground for peanuts, using off-the-shelf equipment and software.

Back in Washington, I do share the wish of public interest groups that public information be made available in electronic form for free—we've already paid for it with taxes. Any document printed by the Government Printing Office (GPO) that currently lands in government document repositories more than likely exists in electronic form (since it was created on a word processor). On-line availability of this information can make students and concerned citizens feel more connected to Washington without placing undue burdens on the government. By restricting access to government agencies or charging high fees (as seems to have happened to a lot of GPO publications in the last decade), the information barons in Washington only intensify the differences between information haves and have-nots.

Myth #7 "The information superhighway will never affect me."

Perhaps by now you have a conflicting view about how the information superhighway will affect you and your family. On the one hand, conventional wisdom and experience indicates that the dream won't be fully realized for perhaps ten to fifteen years. On the other hand, it's quite possible that you feel as though you've already missed the ride on the highway, what with all the news stories that give the impression we're already living at a 21st-century technology level.

The mere fact that you're reading this book means that at least the talk of the information superhighway has affected you in some way. It has aroused curiosity, perhaps fear or intimidation. Yet despite all the hype, none of us "ain't seen nothing yet." Thus the original question: Will the information superhighway affect you, or can you duck the issue?

It's safe to say that if not the highway *per se*, then the stuff that will run on the highway will eventually touch virtually every individual in modern society. This touch won't come to everyone at once, nor can any timetable accurately be presented today. Factors that affect how rapidly the highway and its contents will become a part of your life depend on where you live (country and community) and your occupation.

Occupation plays a big role in how quickly the information superhighway will reach you, because the highway is quickly acquiring on-ramps to businesses and schools. Work and school are the places where you will likely first come into contact with advances in digital communications.

At Work

On the business side, improvements in person-to-person communication and potential savings offered by accompanying technologies make corporate investment in highway on-ramps worthwhile. They literally pay for themselves, much like any investment in people and equipment. For example, the California Department of Transportation (Caltrans), which, among other things, is in charge of the state's road building and maintenance, has already begun to hold meetings of its far-flung staffs via videoconferencing. Instead of having to travel to a centralized meeting location, participants see each other in a video face-to-face group meeting from their respective regions. Fifteen offices spread across the state are set up for videoconferencing. Savings in transportation and other travel costs, plus time savings in trying to schedule all parties, are compelling reasons to adopt this particular communications technology. Caltrans employees who take part in these meetings are being affected by one component of the information superhighway. They may not realize it, because their attention is focused on the meeting content—and that's good. All of the information superhighway should be as subtle when it paves its way into our lives.

Videoconferencing is also in use to enhance medical care available to rural areas. For example, in Giddings, Texas, patients at a small rural clinic can be examined by a specialist fifty-five miles away in Austin. In the clinic room the patient sees two video monitors, one of the remote doctor, the other of what the doctor sees of the patient. A nurse or general practitioner present with the patient talks with the distant specialist while conducting an examination. Unlike in a telephone-voice-only linkup, the remote doctor can see the patient reacting to the exam and make determinations that could not be possible by voice communication only. The patient benefits from having the counsel of a physician who would infrequently or perhaps never travel to that rural facility. The doctor also benefits by being able to treat more patients in far less time. Travel time and expense become nonissues in wide-area treatment.

Working Away from "Work"

Videoconferencing isn't the only technology that demonstrates the effect of the information superhighway on the working world. Telecommuting—the ability to work at a location other than the central office—is already a common practice for millions of knowledge workers in the United States. Obviously some jobs—such as service jobs dealing with customers who venture out into the real world for shopping and entertainment—don't lend themselves to telecommuting. But the majority of automobiles that clog the real highways and pollute urban air travel to and from work during rush hours, carrying plenty of workers who could skip the commute yet still put in a full day's work. Employees whose primary tasks are computer and/or telephone based can perform that work virtually anywhere phone lines run. To accommodate this kind of work from afar, companies must often modify their computer and telephone setups a bit, but the costs are usually nominal compared to those of training new employees who can stomach the commute.

Working out of the office takes on many forms. It could mean working from home, from a small satellite office closer to home than the main office, or from a self-contained office in your car or briefcase if you work "in the field." Typical tools for telecommuters are the telephone and personal computer (equipped with a telephone modem, which allows the computer to communicate with electronic mail and other main office computer services via standard telephone lines). Depending on your communication needs, a fax machine and pager may also be part of the arsenal (although personal computers can handle fax tasks these days without much difficulty).

The Los Angeles earthquake of 1994 hit many knowledge workers and their employers very hard. In that megalopolis, commutes of one or more hours each way in normal circumstances had been common. But when the earth shook enough to close major highways for months, each one-hour trip took two or three hours. To help employees whose jobs were already suited to telecommuting, a number of companies allowed them to work from home or satellite offices for part of each week.

Adapting to Telecommuting

People react differently to telecommuting. Some like the idea of working from home, because it gives them a chance to be near their young children during the day. Many workers with young families find that this has a very positive effect on their productivity and attitude toward their employers. Studies also indicate that home workers tend to be more productive on the days they're at home than on the days they're in the office. Rather than slacking off, they're getting more done, probably because they are subjected to fewer unnecessary interruptions and meaningless meetings.

Working on your own also requires self-discipline. Not everyone has it. Lots of people wouldn't get much done without their co-workers or boss watching over their shoulders or cubicle dividers to keep their noses to the grindstone. Those who have difficulty working on their own may not welcome a policy that mandates telecommuting one or two days each week. Therefore it's questionable how successful some cities, such as Phoenix, will be in their moves to draft legislation requiring local companies and government offices to adopt telecommuting plans for their employees.

The Road Warrior

If you travel a lot in your work—even if just in a car around your city—you are probably already relying on the telephone, voice mail, and perhaps computer every day. For you, wireless technologies will be the most important factor affecting the way you work. Cellular voice-only telephones will become as antiquated as the pay phone is today. In addition to being able to feel connected to the wired world via a wireless link, you will find yourself responding to competitive pressures in your line of work by welcoming new ways to receive information during the day without having to sacrifice human contact time. To that end, personal communicators, such as the Motorola Envoy, and cellular modems for laptop computers will begin to change the way you expect to have information available to you. Such devices will connect to on-line services, pulling down up-to-the-minute information from various sources— newswires, office computers, e-mail boxes—while you're busy driving or meeting with customers. At your leisure, you'll browse through the information that arrived since your last free moment. You will be able to specify that only mail marked "urgent" be sent to your mobile device, both to keep connect time costs to a minimum and to help you sift through tons of daily information for just those items that you have time for. By the same token, these kinds of devices will make you appear even more powerful and professional in front of clients. Instead of saying you'll dash a note to so-and-so to take care of the problem, you can compose a fax on a PDA at the lunch table with your client, tap a button on the screen, and have the fax reach its destination before the next course arrives.

Even if you're not wireless right away, you can have the same facilities by dialing into your mailbox or sending faxes at a pay telephone wired to accept a portable computer's or PDA's modem—an increasingly common sight at business locations (airports, hotels, and convention centers). As with cellular phones, you will make the decision to change from wired to wireless when lack of access to a wire jeopardizes your competitive edge—when you miss a big deal or deadline, for example. You won't allow yourself to be trapped in a pay phone line at a conference or trade show ever again.

The Dollar Value of Time

In business, time is money. When facilities provided by the information superhighway save time, they save you or your company money. Thus, whatever benefits and negatives the superhighway affords will more likely reach you at your work than anywhere else. What you see and when you get it, however, depends on so many factors—the business your employer is in, the competitive climate of that business, the kind of job you have, the financial status of the company, the technological vision top management has, available telecommunications services at your employer's location—that it's foolish to speak of any kind of wave or massive rollout of these technologies. Regardless of your personal desire to adopt the highway's benefits, implementation will be uneven. Two people with the same job at different companies in the same town may not reach technological parity for many years, if ever.

On the consumer side of the highway lane marker, additional factors make the potential adoption of the information superhighway even more uneven. To attract the widest possible audience for home-oriented MIE, the cost must be ridiculously low. Equipment must be truly easy to use and acronym light. There must also be extremely compelling reasons to bring these technologies into the home or our roving pockets.

Target Consumer Markets

A common term in the consumer technology industries is "early adopter." This not so mythical individual is someone who not only enjoys new technology, but is generally willing to pay top dollar for a product's first generation. Supposedly the rest of the consumer market falls into a second, catch-all category. A more detailed division of the consumer marketplace has been proposed by the market research firm Decision Resources Inc., which divides American households into five groups:

> Innovators
> Early Adopters
> Early Majority
> Late Majority
> Low Income and Luddites

Innovators and early adopters (estimated to represent 500,000 and 5 million U.S. households, respectively) are the ones who determine whether a product will succeed. While an innovator might buy even a speculative technology as long as it seems "cool," an early adopter will more likely look for some practical rationale to back up the fact that the technology is cool. Both categories consist of upper-income households, consumers who don't mind being pioneers, even if they're the ones with arrows sticking out of their wallets. In my own experience I've seen this distinction between the two types of households on the leading edge of any technological curve. Innovators bought the first Betamax VCRs, CD players, and Sharp Wizard personal organizers (even if their employers wouldn't let them write off the purchase as an expense). Early adopters took their cues from the innovators they knew, provided they were satisfied with the vision that the technology could bring: time-shifting video recording; seemingly flawless, long-term audio playback; and handy personal information in the pocket.

If it weren't for innovators and early adopters, the prices for nifty gadgets would never come down. Demand from these two segments, according to Decision Resources' scheme, is sufficient to begin the downward spiral of manufacturing costs. As prices lower, and, when conflicting standards exist, a single standard begins to emerge (as with VHS over Beta videocassette formats), the early majority, comprising nearly 35 million households, starts participating in the technology.

The biggest chunk of the market, however, is the late majority—up to 50 million households. This group will adopt a new product or service once it is cheap and demonstrably useful. Decision Resources' definition of "cheap" is below $400. I'm not sure you can place a dollar amount on the threshold that attracts the late majority. It has more to do with value than a hard dollar figure. A technology and device that looks and feels complex, such as the VCR, generally gains mainstream acceptance when low-end models start appearing below the $400 mark. But for items that *seem* less sophisticated (regardless of their actual complexity), that threshold is much lower. For CD players, the flood started, I believe, when prices dipped below $300. Video game machines, even comparatively sophisticated ones, are a hard sell above $200.

The Dribbleware and Standards Factors

While this consumer market model is instructive—have you determined where you fit?—it's unclear whether it will apply for the aggregate of the information superhighway. Unlike a technology such as the VCR, compact audio disc, or even the microwave oven, the information superhighway isn't product oriented. You can't buy it in a store, or tell your friends to buy one, even if you have the facilities at your home and like to show off. Because of the uneven geographical distribution of a number of information superhighway access roads—cable and wireless, in particular—innovators might be the sole highway consumers in one community or region, while in another place not far away, suppliers of information superhighway stuff might already be attracting the early majority.

In past technology revolutions, standards have played a significant role. So it was with audiocassettes displacing eight-track tapes, VHS displacing Beta, and today with the inability of several alternate audio formats (digital audio tape, digital compact cassette, and minidisc) to make headway against the compact audio disc juggernaut. It's still unclear how important standards that affect users will play on the information superhighway. For strictly telephone-based services, service providers will supply personal computer software for the standard operating systems, such as Macintosh and Windows (in whatever generations). As new operating systems gain strength in numbers—OS/2, Windows NT, Taligent, Magic Cap—the services will likely provide software for machines running those platforms as well. It would obviously be easier for them if there were a single personal computing standard (or even just a few), but service providers, unfortunately, are in an aftermarket position. People sign up for their services after purchasing a computer; rarely do they buy a computer just to sign up for the service.

Delivery of other kinds of information, especially for set-top box scenarios, causes standards problems for the information and multimedia designers, but not so much for the consumers. If it should evolve that there is no competition for your attention from multiple providers on the same cable, then there will be no standards issue for you: you'll have to use the set-top box that is compatible with the cable service to which you are connected. That box's internal design will depend largely on the nature of the setup of the cable office. Some boxes may be able to store temporarily lots of video and other information; in other instances the cable office (or somewhere in between) will do the storage and your box will merely "dial it up." You won't be buying the box, of course. Rather, the cable company will build the rental cost into monthly service contracts or find some other way to get households to pay off the initial cost of the box. Therefore it's no skin off your teeth if your box isn't compatible with your sister's set-top box in the next state. When you move across the country, you'll turn in your first box, and get a new one at the cable office near your new home.

One standard that you will be interested in, however, is content. Today, when you travel around the United States, you expect to be able to receive the national broadcast networks from any television set in every motel from Maine to Hawaii. You probably don't expect that of the cable lineup you may have plugged into your home. But if you have cable at home and in your motel room, you may expect some standards, such as CNN and ESPN, to be available. That's not always the case. Fortunately, few people rely heavily on the content of broadcast or cable television. But if the information superhighway is to attract a mass audience with content, that content will have to be so compelling that you'd feel lost without it. What happens when you travel to New Orleans, for example, and find that your vital information service isn't available there? Or, what happens if you use your cable TV provider as a gateway for electronic messaging and the cable provider at your travel destination doesn't have such a gateway? You may not even have a personal computer or other device to connect to what has become an important person-to-person lifeline for you: electronic mail.

The Roaming Warrior

The same goes for travelers who rely on wireless access. In this case, the standards issue is one of access to a particular data carrier, whose system operates on a government-allocated swath of the radio spectrum. You must hope that either the same carrier operates in other parts of the country (or world?) or that there are cooperative arrangements with carriers of the same service on the same frequencies at your destination. Cellular telephone users today have problems with this in many cases as it is. While it is possible to "roam" to another service area, setting up roaming upon arrival in another area can take a bit of dialing work for the system to recognize your phone and to instruct your home system to forward incoming calls to you in the other service area. Strangely enough, a cellular phone contains enough data about their owner to automatically tell a different carrier in a new town how to handle the roaming setup. The computers running most cellular systems, however, aren't up to the task quite yet. For nomadic digital data to be a reality, roaming must become invisible and seamless to the user.

Existing wireless systems, however, cause problems when users travel to other countries. Few regions of the world use the same frequency allocations or channel schemes for cellular telephone service. Therefore it's useless to bring a U.S. cellular phone on a trip with you outside North America. It is also unlikely that ground-based wireless telephone and digital data services will allow for global roaming within our lifetime. In fact, the problem of coordinating services in different countries is so severe that some companies are bypassing the problem entirely and looking to the sky for the solution. Instead of our wireless devices linking up with antennas mounted on tall buildings and towers, they'll be communicating directly with low-orbit satellites. With enough satellites circling the globe (not in geosynchronous orbits, as most television and long-haul telecom networks are), virtually every square inch of the planet will be reachable via wireless voice and data at every second of the day. Motorola plans to begin launching its Iridium network of 66 satellites in 1996. Loral Corp. and Hughes Aircraft Co. have satellite network plans of their own. Meanwhile, a startup company called Teledesic proposed in March 1994 a monster network of 840 satellites intended more for rural areas or other parts of the world where wire-line service is difficult to obtain. Subscribing to these or other similar services—should their deployment live up to their promises—would alleviate the standards issue for wireless devices. The nice thing about wireless devices, including those as "primitive" as today's analog voice cellular telephones, is that they eventually connect to the wireline world. Once you have dial tone, you can reach a huge world of people, computers, and other devices—if someone or something has a telephone number, you can reach him, her, or it.

As stated before, you are more likely to first come into contact with the information superhighway outside your home. What will probably happen, as is now happening for personal computers, is that you'll become so dependent on the communications aspects of the highway—certainly for messaging and information—that you'll feel naked when you come home and don't have those facilities.

A Consumer Target

Even if you're not in a hurry to ride on the highway from your easy chair, the demographics of your household may make you an early target, provided you have access to the services via phone (and computer) or cable company. And when service providers reach your area, you can be sure you'll be hit with all kinds of offers—test programs, trial subscriptions, charter memberships, you name it. Moreover, if according to census statistics you live in an upper-income area, you are more likely to fall in the innovator and early adopter categories. That makes you a prime target for the services. Even if you're not interested, you'll be hammered by the direct marketing efforts aimed squarely at your household. So, yes, even if you consider yourself an information highway Luddite, you will be affected—if not by the highway itself, then by the promotion and hype to get you to ride along.

Among the appeals will be those that try to tug at your heartstrings. You may have already seen the television advertisements from Motorola, which has entered the consumer market for pagers. In addition to creating models in neon colors, the company shows in its ads how this technology can help strengthen the bonds among family members. Kids trapped in the rain after a canceled ball game use their emergency pay phone money to ring Mom's pager. In the next scene, Mom shows up to rescue the kids from the wrath of Mother Nature. In the same commercial, parents of a young child relish the fact that they're going out for the evening, while leaving the kid in the hands of a baby-sitter who has the parents' pager number.

I expect we'll see a variety of advertisements directed at each constituency in the house. Just as today television commercials are often directed at kids to get their parents to buy toys and games, so too will the highway-hype ads entice kids to beg parents for *its* "product"—access to interactive games. Parents will be shown how their children will be able to get ahead in the world with access to libraries of information. Later, as wireless technologies become cheaper, the personal security issue will loom large in advertising. Between the news media's recent emphasis on violent crime and the availability of wireless services, we'll all want a 911-equipped voice communicator cum global positioning satellite receiver built into our wristwatches.

Oh, yes, we'll all be affected by the information super-highway, whether we ride it or not.

Myth #8 "I will be crushed under tons of information arriving via the superhighway."

If all the world's computers were, in fact, linked together in one information superhighway, a healthy percentage of everything that is known on planet Earth about the universe would be on tap. Even within the confines of a single service provider of today's scale, the amount of information is overwhelming. The amorphous, anarchic web that is linked together via the Internet is the most promising and at the same time frightening information collection of all. Few creative media are being left out of the rush to digitize every new idea, text chunk, video run, sound string, or image snapshot. Moreover, the global web of linked computers makes it possible for virtually anyone to publish anything (although not necessarily get paid for the work). Marketplace filters—editors, publishers, media producers—no longer serve as gatekeepers to individual communicators. In an ideal, altruistic world, all these digital bits would be available to anyone with the equipment to retrieve and decode them.

Overload Trends

Many of those who use electronic mail in their work have experienced the feeling of digital overload, just with the number of messages that appear in their in-boxes each day. It's not uncommon for a well-connected, e-mail intensive company to load managers' mailboxes with more than a hundred messages each day. Not all of the messages are important. Lots of messages to others are copied to someone "for your information." Also, the ability to broadcast messages to groups of employees at once means that some messages may be from the receptionist alerting the company that a particular vehicle in the parking lot has its lights on or someone is selling a baby carriage.

In the hunt for news reports in the telecommunications field for this book, I used the search facilities of a few commercial on-line services. Even though I could limit my searches by keywords, it was not uncommon for the computer to come back with more than one hundred references from a variety of sources. Anyone researching today's hot topics—biotechnology, government policy, environmental and ecological sciences, world geopolitics—would be equally overwhelmed by the quantity of new information available each day. What boggles the mind and leads to the myth of premature burial by information is that the amount of information flowing on today's information wagon trails is just a trickle compared with what will probably flow when the highways reach hundreds of millions of people around the world.

Perhaps because the engineers of the information superhighway are themselves overwhelmed today, there is a heightened sensitivity to the potential for the deluge of information discouraging most people from taking part in the information highway. Many of these same engineers are equipped to turn the computers that cause the problem into the tools that will solve the problem. For in addition to the flood of information coming toward you, the distribution of this information among potentially millions of computers around the world make it just as difficult to find information you are interested in. Today, the kinds of tools we can begin to use include software technologies known as *filters* and *agents*.

Filtering Electronic Mail

Let's take the example of the 100-plus e-mail message executive. In practice, a great percentage of electronic mail messages that are targeted to an individual become to-do list items. The messages request action on the part of the recipient, whether it be to prepare some data for a superior or share knowledge in the form of a reply. When pressed for time, a manager wants to distill from the hundred messages just those that need attention for immediate reading. Copies of messages sent to others can usually wait, and the "for sale" announcements can be overlooked. Among the messages that require some action, clearly some requests—those from superiors, for example—take priority.

At the leading edge of available in-house electronic mail systems today are those that let recipients define rules for filtering incoming messages. For example, you could instruct your intelligent mailbox to sort incoming messages such that all mail addressed to you alone (as opposed to you among several others in a distribution list) and originating from individuals in the levels of management above you is always placed at the top of your in-box. Other rules may group all mail coming to you as a copy in a special electronic folder that you've named "FYI" or automatically delete all messages with the words *for sale* in the subject line.

Filter Hazards

E-mail filters unfortunately can have adverse side effects. For example, if your filters are set so tightly that they allow mail from only a small subset of people on your mail system to reach your in-box, you may never receive what could be an important missive from someone outside the circle you've created. The democracy that electronic mail encourages—in the mail system, each message is merely a compilation of bits—is diminished by filters.

Electronic Alter Egos

An even more powerful concept to help manage large amounts of information is the software agent. Like a human agent, a software agent operates in the background on your behalf. The term, however, is often overused by companies creating software that performs any action on behalf of a human user. Even among experts, a precise definition is difficult to come by. Some would argue that the mail filtering process described above is an agent-run process. Others would suggest that a true agent also represents the user in communication back to the sender. Therefore, an e-mail agent might not only forward your mail to an associate while you're on vacation, but also send a note back to senders saying that you are away and that the messages are being passed to your associate.

Impressive as this kind of agent process may be, other technologies, which should be in place by the end of 1994, take software agentry further. General Magic, a company founded by a number of Apple Computer alumni (and funded initially by Apple), has created a software technology called Telescript. Users of computers don't ever really see Telescript operating, but they do see the results. Telescript is a programming language for programs that run on large computers controlling commercial on-line services (and private systems in the future). An on-line service, such as AT&T PersonaLink Services, has its main computers equipped to run Telescript programs. These programs are planted inside the central computers by users' personal computers or personal communicators. Telescript programs—agents—perform operations for the human user while the human user is not connected to the service.

Running Errands for You

In addition to filtering and forwarding of e-mail messages, Telescript agents can do much more, provided the on-line service can run those agents. For example, without connecting to an on-line service, you can use some friendly software on your personal communicator to establish an itinerary for a business trip next week. You specify the dates and times for the flights and the destination. While your interaction is limited to tapping a few buttons on the screen with a stylus and typing a few characters, you are actually instructing your personal communicator to create a Telescript agent. Upon connecting to the on-line service, your personal communicator transfers the agent to the main computer, starts the agent, and disconnects from the main computer. In that agent is your credit card information (encrypted) and other pertinent data that an agent making flight reservations would need to know.

While you're busy doing something else, your electronic agent connects to a flight reservation service, locates flights that meet your time schedule, books the reservation (even paying for the tickets with your credit card), and sends you an e-mail message with confirmation data. Even that e-mail message has agentlike powers, because the note will ask you if you want to insert the flight data into the calendar that is kept in your personal communicator. A tap of the Yes button makes that happen.

Now comes the day of your flight. The Telescript agent that placed your reservation is still alive on the main computer. Three hours prior to scheduled departure, it contacts the airline reservation system again, checking for on-time departure. If the flight is delayed, the Telescript agent sends you an urgent e-mail message (or perhaps an alphanumeric message to your pager) to alert you of the new scheduled departure time.

In yet another example of how an agent can work for you, let's say you want to find out everything that has been published about a particular company within the last sixty days. You may not even know where all the information exists. But a number of commercial information services have search programs of their own that can locate databases containing the information you need. By sending your agent out to these services, it can query the depths of each service, trolling the world for data. After gathering all the information it could find, the agent places the data in a word-processing document and e-mails the document to you. Later that day you download that document and read through it. In this case the agent was a valuable research assistant. You may never know or care what computer the information was found on.

Similar agentlike processes can create a customized newspaper for you each morning. Culling through various published on-line sources, the agent can assemble articles that relate to specific companies, industries, or interests that you've defined by keywords. By the time you check your mail first thing in the morning, your custom newspaper is ready for you.

Agent Hazards

Agents that do this kind of filtering and directed work for humans bring with them just as many attendant problems as electronic mail filters. I mention this to debate an insightful observation made by Nicholas Negroponte, founder of the MIT Media Lab. In a speech he gave at a conference in February 1994, he stated his ideas about how our attention spans differ at various times during the week. For example, during working hours of a busy week, we have limited time to deal with information. Therefore we tend to focus on just the important items that need attention—the kind of items that manage to bore their way through our filters. At other times of the week, such as on Sunday, we have more time to browse information.

While I agree with this notion wholeheartedly, I don't believe that it takes into account how software agents can potentially close our minds to new ideas. If our entire information flow comes from the information superhighway, and we establish filters and agents to grab only the stuff we tell them to, we define limits for ourselves that may never be broken. Invariably, the amount of information even within the confines of our filters begins to build. After a while we either narrow the filters some more or manually handle only the really important stuff during the busy times, leaving less important items for the time used normally for casual browsing.

I've seen this happen in my own experience with on-line services. Admittedly I subscribe to more than my share of services, but I find that I get into patterns of forums and other areas that I visit on a regular basis. Some of those areas cover recreational interests that are important to the psyche. But when the crush is on during the week, I'll skip some of those forums and instead just do a quick check to see if anyone has sent me any e-mail or left me messages on those forums. Casual browsing time is devoted—less frequently, of course—to spending more time in those forums, reading threads. I stick to those patterns almost invariably, leaving to explore another area only if something triggers an interest or question along the way. In this on-line medium, my patterns (and agents in the future) limit my browsing.

Contrast that kind of browsing with sitting down with the Sunday *New York Times*. Sitting in my lap is a world of information from a variety of sources, covering more topics than I would ever think to explore. I'll read in depth about the political turmoil in some faraway country that doesn't make the headlines during the week. Or there may be an interesting story about a personal triumph, an op-ed piece by Vaclav Havel, the weekly automobile column, book reviews on subjects I didn't realize I find interesting. For all practical purposes, I have assigned the agent job to the editorial staff of the newspaper. While not tailoring the content of the edition to my specific desires, the editors have aimed to satisfy the general desires of its customer base—of which I have elected to be a member on any given Sunday. On the other hand, a software agent whose knowledge I define will be no smarter than I am. It will take the technology developments of many lifetimes before software agents have the intelligence to infer what their human owners *might* want to know. In the meantime, relying on agents to do all our information work for us will gradually close us off from new ideas and new interests. We'll still need occasionally to rely on the agentry of those we trust, such as a newspaper or magazine editorial staff, to allow for occasional diversity. Information overload may be less of a concern than the possibility that technology may close us off from a variety of information.

Navigating through Information

The question remains: How will we navigate through large collections of information, such as those currently found on systems linked through the Internet? On-screen text menus and icons have inherent limitations in that they can display only so much information on a screen at a time. Moreover, such screens on commercial services tend to be designed in ways that don't reveal much about the true relationships of collections of information.

In earlier discussions about the Internet, I mentioned the World Wide Web. One feature of a WWW on-screen document is its ability to display highlighted text that leads to a screen of related information when you click a mouse pointer on it. The related information can come from another computer literally on the other side of the planet. The links, of course, are established by the screen document's writers, but this manner of *hypertext* linking eases navigation to a large degree.

Even more exciting, experimental work at MIT Media Lab is quite extraordinary in its explorations of displaying information collections in a three-dimensional space. This is a difficult concept to describe in words or demonstrate with anything less than full animation (ah, the limits of the printed page!), but when you see some of the experiments in motion, the concepts begin to make a great deal of sense.

To visualize a three-dimensional information space, imagine that you're floating in mid-air. Off in the distance you might see the title of a book that intrigues you. As you propel yourself toward the book title, whose text floats in space, you begin to see more details about the book (like a table of contents) behind the title. The closer you come to this book's information space, the more you see about it. Flying like Commando Cody, you dive deeper into the information, seeing individual chapter titles and then text and graphics within each chapter. Perhaps there is a reference to another work elsewhere in the information space. A literal thread connects that point of information where you are to the other work. After flying along that thread, you reach the other work, also displayed in three-dimensional space. You view this information space on the video screen while controlling your location by a device such as a joystick. By wearing a virtual reality helmet, you could actually see this information world in 3-D and fly toward something that interests you from afar by pointing with a wired, gloved hand.

This sounds pretty farfetched, I know. But when I saw the demonstrations of these very early concept prototypes, it was a revelation—not in the precise examples of what the demos showed, but in what I imagined as the potential for creating three-dimensional models for the world of information. If these kinds of tools help everyday information users visualize where their information comes from and how it is related to other information, then information providers may find it easier to assemble the world's raw data into new knowledge that can benefit users.

In the near term, as the general public gains access to a rapidly increasing web of information, the threat of information overload is more real than myth. But the problem is one that can eventually be managed by computer software. Filters and agents will serve us well initially, but even more sophisticated systems will come along to help us navigate through immense information collections with relative ease.

Myth #9 The information superhighway will create a world of hermits and loners.

A lot of the thinking surrounding this myth must come from looking at today's cloistered personal computer hobbyists and video game junkies and envisioning tomorrow's highway riders. The stereotypes are perhaps justly earned, but if that's the model of future passengers on the information superhighway, we can close the road right now.

Virtual Communities—Real People

The truth is, those who already use on-line services spend a great deal of time in the forums and conference areas communicating with other users. Not all conversation is in real time—members leave bulletin-board-style messages for each other like notes at a student union cork board—but these users are hardly disconnecting from the world.

The on-line messaging world amply supports the views that the human being is a "social animal" (Demetrius, A.D. first century) or "formed for society" (Sir William Blackstone, eighteenth century). Each individual's response to an electronic encounter is different. Whether the cyberspace of choice is a local bulletin board, a commercial service, or the massive Internet world (predominantly the newsgroup portion), you can elect to get as involved with others as you like. In fact, for newcomers there is a level of anonymous voyeurism that serves as a healthy introduction to these services. Unlike the cocktail party loaded with people you don't know, an electronic forum allows you to observe exchanges among others in the group while those folks don't even know you're tracking the conversation (conversely, by posting their conversations in public, they have no expectation of privacy and may even hope that people with additional views will join in). For the "lurker," as this kind of browser is called, there is no awkward feeling that contribution is mandatory—you don't have to jump in until you're ready to do so.

If you frequent one or more forums on a regular basis, especially if you exchange ideas with others from time to time, you begin to get to know the likes and dislikes of active people on the forum. Before long you will probably sense a community feeling, which is why these electronic groups are called virtual communities. When the group is spread over great distances geographically, it is possible you will never communicate with the regulars by any other method, nor will you meet them face-to-face. Thus a virtual community has all aspects of community except for physical contact among its members.

Stories of virtual communities coming together to help their fellow citizens are legend. They include people coming to the financial rescue of members who find themselves in dire straits due to illness. As in any human community, death removes members from the active ranks. On-line wakes for beloved forum members are not uncommon. Members in more closely knit forums get moral support from each other in times of family or other personal crisis.

Author Howard Rheingold documents much of this activity in his book *The Virtual Community* (1993, Addison

Wesley). Howard is a member of an on-line group whose members live mostly in the San Francisco Bay area. Called the WELL (Whole Earth 'Lectronic Link), it not only provides forums of local interest, but also provides access to the Internet. For some on-line folks the physical community adds to the virtual one, when members do, in fact, meet for parties and picnics around San Francisco. If you haven't experienced the feeling before, it's quite odd entering a roomful of real people whose faces you couldn't pick out of a police lineup yet whose inner beings you may feel you know intimately from on-line conversations. It happens not only among local BBS users, but even at professional conferences, when you meet face-to-face people with whom you've carried on many conversations on-line about business or other common interests.

Wireless data communications just now reaching the business world in force also encourage human-to-human contact, even if that contact is not in real time or face-to-face. The fact that an entire class of wireless devices are called personal *communicators* indicates that we yearn to be in touch with others. The technology lets us communicate on our own terms; we decide when and where the contact takes place. That's why we often let the answering machine catch an incoming call when we've just sat down to dinner. Or we go out to the mailbox to see what has arrived via snail mail when we're ready to deal with that incoming communication. The handy-dandy wireless communicator will encourage us to be in contact with more people more often, as we extend our personal virtual communities.

The Limits of Text

But even this warm-and-fuzzy world of virtual community has potential downsides. A lot of it has to do with the text medium that predominates on-line exchanges today. Also playing a role is the fact that people tend to be less inhibited on-line than if they were conversing with the same people over a cup of coffee.

As mentioned in the framework of electronic mail, electronic text messages are very democratic. They bear no logo, trademark, fancy letterhead, or high-resolution laser printout to distinguish the class of its originator. Some of the biggest computer industry luminaries are known to all fellow on-line participants by their first names. The less you know about a person in the real world, the more likely you are to greet that person on equal footing, even if the two of you are are of completely different ages, occupations, and economic and education levels. Literacy, however, still counts if you want others to understand what you're trying to say—hence my contention earlier that literacy will play a big role in distinguishing haves from have-nots on the information highway. You are judged primarily on your ideas, knowledge, humor, and general contribution to the sense of community within any forum. It's not uncommon to be an expert in one area and a complete rookie in another. Each of the communities consists of an entirely different group of people. Just as you might circulate around a big party, in some conversation circles you may be the center of attention, while in others you defer to those who seem to have the floor.

But if electronic text messages are democratic, they are also one-dimensional means of communicating ideas. In live face-to-face contact with another person, there is a lot of body language, and other communication comes from the intonation of your voice. What you might voice with a chuckle of sarcasm may be read from the silent screen as a smart-aleck crack that offends the recipient.

Igniting Flames

Misinterpreting expressions is a fairly common occurrence in the virtual community, except where the participants know each other extremely well. A newcomer, for example, might ask a harmless question that has been asked hundreds of times before. An expert may flash back an answer along with a crack that makes the newcomer feel like a real rube. It's hardly the welcome wagon. That newcomer may either flee in terror, never to return, or harbor some ill feelings toward the know-it-all jerk, who could more politely direct the "newbie" to a file containing answers to frequently asked questions (FAQs).

Messages that lash out at other people, ideas, and events are so common that the on-line world has a special name for them (mentioned previously): *flames*. People who send such messages on a regular basis are called *flamers*. For some, flaming is a kind of therapy, an outlet to vent some frustration or other anger. Unfortunately, unsuspecting recipients of flames can take the messages personally. I can't count the number of times that message threads have turned away from the subject to talk about the perceived and real personal attacks that participants get involved with. When someone flames you, it sometimes seems that the more you try to defend yourself, the higher the flamer turns up the heat.

I'm convinced that some people in the on-line world truly enjoy being royal pains. On one of the commercial services I regularly hook up, there is an individual whose message threads I don't even bother contributing to. His expertise is parsing the grammar and logic of each response—in a medium where the quick, unedited message is the norm. Within only a couple of exchanges with this guy, you're spending all your time defending *how* you said something, rather than *what* you said. After a while, longtime community members know who the regular flamers are, and you'll get an occasional private message of support in your battle against the known flamer.

Text with Emotion

To head off potential misinterpretations, a number of conventions have arisen to communicate emotions or sarcasm along with plain text. One method is to insert a <g> symbol after your remark, indicating that you are grinning while typing it. As the recipient reads along, the blood may begin to boil, until the <g> removes the pot from the stove. Another way to avoid misunderstanding is to use one of the common abbreviations that alerts the reader that a statement is an opinion. The abbreviation is IMHO, which stands for "in my humble opinion." Even if the opinion isn't humble, it still defuses what otherwise might come across as a statement of universal truth, which will surely bring out of the woodwork people who disagree with the statement. The easiest way to appear like a flamer is to denigrate that which another person on the forum worships. Stating that something is stupid, dumb, the best, the worst, a waste of time, or ludicrous will definitely get a response. If you temper the statement with IMHO, it may be taken as an opinion to which you are entitled.

Even more common these days are strange-looking text symbols, called *emoticons* or *smileys*, whose interpretations are best understood by looking at them sideways. The smiley that conveys the simple grin is :-). Tilt your head to the left ninety degrees; see how the colon represents the eyes, the hyphen the nose, and the right parenthesis the smile? A large library of smileys is in common use. There's even *Smiley Dictionary* (Peachpit Press), published to help you master these symbols of subtlety. The need for these symbols came from the fact that even in cyberspace, IMHO, humans are social animals. When the technology of text limits body language and voice inflection, we seek ways to convey as much of our humanness as we can within the medium. That would seem to be a sign of our desire to participate in community, rather than withdraw from it.

Beyond Text

As the number of lanes on the superhighway increases, it's possible that virtual community members won't be trapped in a text-only world. Audio and video exchanges may supplement or replace text messages. Seeing and/or hearing others in the virtual community may destroy or alter cyberspace's democracy, because members will likely exhibit the same prejudices toward their on-line contacts that they do toward people they meet face to face. The characteristics that text messages hide—age, race, looks, accent, and sometimes gender—will draw some people closer together, pull others further apart. Will the messages—people's ideas—be eclipsed by physical window dressing? We may learn, after all, that text, despite its inherent hazards, is the medium that brings us closest together in a virtual community.

Myth #10 "I can't possibly watch five hundred channels!"

Stories about five hundred channels of cable television streaming into our homes are humdingers. I don't think I've ever heard so many respected journalists (and plenty I don't respect) jump to the most idiotic conclusions based on a single technology announcement. The truth, however, is not so exciting, so perhaps it was important to create a bit of news for the sake of their audiences.

More Filling, Less Taste

At the root of this phenomenon are technologies that will make it possible to broadcast five hundred discrete channels of video entertainment to a community cable system. All that's at stake here is bandwidth—how many compressed video signals can be sent simultaneously. Somehow journalists confused this potential with actual programming possibilities. Let's do some quick arithmetic to see how ridiculous this proposition is.

Today, roughly sixty million homes in the United States are connected to cable systems. Assuming that today a) all households had access to five hundred-channel cable systems; b) five hundred channels of programming were available; and c) at any given instant every household was watching at least one channel—the average viewership per channel would be a paltry (in TV ratings) 120,000 households. Of course, viewers distribution would be unequal, since many more people would be watching the 1996 summer Olympics from Atlanta than would be studying close-up stitches on the Crochet Channel. So the obvious question becomes: How on earth could all those channels afford to stay on the air? Viewers would be willing to pay only so much per month for a specialty channel. On advertiser-supported channels, advertisers would be stretched across so many channels that they couldn't possibly pay for ads on even a tiny fraction of those five hundred channels. Even if a number of channels were devoted to home shopping (and would therefore pay for themselves), how many home shopping channels could survive if potential shoppers were spread out among dozens of competitors? For that matter, why would we even want so many channels dedicated to drawing extra dollars from our pockets for goods? (Ah, for the good old days, when all we had to contend with were junk mail, junk phone calls, and junk faxes!)

Fill in the Blanks

The true problem with this is that we can't yet visualize how those five hundred channels could be used. In an effort to connect with consumers (and investors), cable and technology companies describe the content of those channels in terms of today's services. Therefore, they content us by filling out our channel selection with cable programs not currently carried by our cable service or with channels allocated to staggered video schedules and video-on-demand kinds of services. In one scenario, a number of channels would be set aside for a particular motion picture—usually a pay-per-view offering of a recent film not yet available as a video rental. Rather than airing the film on one channel every couple of hours, the company would start the film on the hour on one channel, start the same film at fifteen past the hour on another channel, and so on, until eight or ten channels are filled with that one movie, each channel having a different start time.

"Video on demand" is also a service touted as a means of filling channels. After viewing a listing of videos available from the local cable office on one channel, you can use your remote control to select a particular film. The cable company would then broadcast that film on a particular channel among the hundreds available for video-on-demand service. As with today's pay-per-view scheme, your selection of film authorizes the rental charge, and the cable company sends a signal with your set-top box's code number so that it descrambles the film delivered on, say, channel 380. Other people on the same cable system can view a list of the other movies playing and how far into the video each channel is. By making the same kind of on-screen menu selection, they can join you in your video, although neither household knows who's watching what.

Convenience vs. Cost

Video on demand has its proponents and naysayers. While it may not be a compelling reason to ride the information super-highway, it can offer significant convenience over the video rental store, and it should be much easier to browse through promotional trailers for films to help you make your selec-tion—something that isn't always possible at the video store. However, if home service providers expect to get more money for this convenience, they're mistaken when it comes to the consumer world. Unless video on demand costs no more than the two or three dollars it currently costs to rent a video, it may not succeed. The cable companies may try to sell you on how much money and time you save by not having to drive to the video store. But unlike time-is-money business activity, I don't believe consumers think of time or convenience as money. Given the choice between a $5.95 video on demand and a $3 one-day rental from the video store, consumers will consider the rental a better buy, even if it does, in fact, cost time and real money to make two trips to the store (for rental and return). The same is true for the current setup in home computer bank-ing. It infuriates me that my bank charges an extra monthly fee for home banking via telephone and personal computer. Since each electronic transaction eliminates human paper processing, the bank should be paying its customers to bank by home computer. Ninety-six dollars per year seems like a lot of money to pay for reducing the bank's processing.

Where's the Channel Selector?

It is doubtful that the huge channel capacity cable systems will be universally installed. As mentioned earlier, the tele-phone switching model of sending just one user-selected channel to the set-top box may be more efficient from a bandwidth point of view. This puts the onus of the "physical" switching on the computers at the central office (just as it's done by your local phone company for voice calls), rather than inside your cable box or television set, as with cable systems in use today. When your local cable company decides that it's time to upgrade the equipment, they'll be asking themselves which route to go. You may end up skipping the cable altogether because a similar service is available over the phone company wire.

In the end, fear not the five hundred-channel cable box. You won't spend almost ten minutes surfing through the channels one channel per second in search of viewable fare. That's not to say the selection won't increase. But when it starts to get out of hand, the video provider's computers will offer ways to help you select from all available programs by sorting programs by content, type, length, currency, or whatever they figure consumers want. Similar aids will likely help in the near term to program our VCRs to catch programs when we can't watch them at airing time. For example, we might look at an on-screen TV guide and select the programs we want to tape by pressing a button on our set-top box remote controller. When the program airs (even if it's delayed by some news special), the video company sends a signal to your set-top box, which in turn instructs your VCR deck to begin recording.

This VCR-in-the-home scenario reminds me a bit of how most of us started out with an answering machine at home. More recently, many local phone companies have upgraded their systems to provide the answering machine function for you inside their computers. The incoming caller leaves a message on the phone company computer in a voice mail in-box. Only someone with your numeric password can retrieve the messages stored there. Similarly, the video program computers at our local information superhighway provider may take over the task of recording programs for us. Once a program airs, we may be able to instruct our set-top box to dig out the program from the local company's computers and play it for us whenever we want. The TV guide will be less of a viewing schedule and more of a release schedule. Once a program is released (aired in its normal time slot), we can view it any time we like.

More information superhighway myths are likely to appear, even after services begin flowing into homes on a regular basis. In the final chapter I'll give you some tips on how to prevent future myths from clouding your judgment about new technologies and services.

CHAPTER FIVE

Out of the Rubble of Old Infrastructures

Within only the past few years, we have seen electronic journalism transform our expectations of instant worldwide access to historic events. Not only do we get a verbal account of the bombing of Baghdad, but a live television camera sticking out of the window of the Al Rashid Hotel shows glowing trails of antiaircraft rounds spraying into the night sky. From our comfy sofas we watch with utter disbelief as a brave young man stands before an oncoming tank on its way to help quash the Tiananmen Square demonstration. Our evening news anchors broadcast their reports live from in front of the Berlin Wall as free citizens literally hammer away at a modern symbol of repression. We're glued to the television with a variety of emotions as flames whip through a religious compound in Waco, Texas.

This kind of instant access meshes well with modern society's culture of more, bigger, better, and faster. At times it seems as though we can't get enough of anything. It reminds me of the market research studies that a young marketing whiz named John Sculley performed years ago while he worked at PepsiCo. The company delivered increasingly larger caches of Pepsi-Cola to its test customers each week. The more the company delivered, the more the families consumed. The more live drama that the news networks provide, the more we watch. The more we can be in touch with people from wherever we are, the more cellular telephones we buy.

Old Infrastructures at the Brink

The crunch comes when we begin demanding more of infrastructures than they can provide. With rare exceptions—mostly electronic communications systems, which are working hard to keep pace with demand—many of the infrastructures we grew up with are under severe strain. The strain has many forms—economic, environmental, even quality of life.

Take the infrastructure known as the public library. Many people look upon the public library as an important part of their own information culture. Yet it seems that public libraries get the short end of the budget stick year after year. Does the town allocate funds for filling potholes this year or replacing the library staff member who retired? It's often that critical in many communities. Branches are closing, hours are being shortened, acquisition of new material is down. It's not uncommon to find a library closed for one day each week in the middle of the week. Many people are discovering that their only source of information on demand, if you will, is drying up.

Public schools are feeling the same kinds of budget crunches. The school day is shortening. Nonacademic courses or activities may be good for the students' souls, but they also break the budget. Creative outlets such as music and art are often the first to go. Sports and other recreational activities are usually next on the list. Student-sponsored fund-raising programs are often required to help purchase equipment like personal computers. In many schools classroom overcrowding reduces the likelihood that students can get personal attention they may need in their studies.

Transportation infrastructures, particularly urban highways, are also under pressure. Traffic during peak hours increases faster than lanes can be added to highways—when lanes can be added at all. As congestion increases, employees waste more hours every week crawling along high-speed arteries. While unleaded gasoline seems to have helped decrease pollution in some cities, the situation won't get better as long as internal combustion engines power virtually every vehicle on the road. In the meantime, commuting vehicles consume a great deal of nonrenewable energy in a most inefficient system—you simply can't get your mileage's worth out of a gallon of gasoline at an average speed of twenty miles per hour.

Quality of life, while not a specific infrastructure that can be built with concrete and steel, also seems to be threatened. Despite official statistics to the contrary, the average U.S. citizen's perception is that violent crime against innocent victims is on the rise. Perhaps the jump in our fears is attributable to increased media coverage of muggings, rape, random violence, gang shootings, and a comparatively new crime category, carjacking, of which the FBI reported a 24 percent increase from 1991 to 1992. People who fled the fear of crime in urban areas now feel as though crime has followed them to suburbia and beyond. Television news frequently provides tips on how to make it safely from the shopping mall store to your car in the parking ramp. We arm ourselves with exposed car keys and concealed pepper spray cans just to buy a pair of shoes. Will the fear of crime eventually make us think twice about even leaving the house for all but essential trips? You couldn't watch the lawlessness and devastation of the Los Angeles riots following the

Rodney King verdict without recalling apocalyptic science fiction movies like *Blade Runner* and *Escape from New York*.

With only so much cash to go around to attempt solutions for these infrastructure overloadings, communications and computing technologists point to possible solutions that their technologies provide for the future. In some cases the technologies are presented as ways of bracing the existing infrastructures to give them extra life; others are aimed at replacing infrastructures that perhaps no longer fit the way we've fashioned our own societies.

Libraries

Those of us who grew up with respect and admiration for the public library's rows and rows of books, volumes of periodicals, and quiet refuge from the outside world may feel it a shame that the institutions as we knew them may disappear over time. In their place will be electronic access to the same—if not better—information. To be utilitarian about it, a library is a warehouse of information. If we can retrieve that same information, not just plain text but complete pages, on high-resolution video screens, at any time of the day or night from our homes or offices, the edifice of the library building becomes irrelevant. And if library collections from many libraries are gathered electronically in (what appears to us as) one computer that lets us search for information across many disciplines and lines of thought, then the library we remember will seem like a horse carriage in a world of supersonic aircraft.

Between this pipedream and today's reality lie variations that are starting to reach the real world. Already a number of libraries publish their catalogs on computers available to Internet users. There are still many problems with issues of copyright and royalty payments for viewing works not in the public domain, so the issue of on-line access to current texts will take some years to work out. Also, printed books may never be displaced completely by electronic books. There is something sensual about the weight of a book in our hands, the texture of the paper, the contrast of the ink on the page, the sense of space you get as you make your way through to the end—how soon will we be willing to give up these things, even if there were highly portable, pocket-size devices that could display book pages for us? Still, electronic books—as exemplified by well-executed interactive multimedia presentations—can provide a much richer experience than a printed book. Therefore a number of new authors may gravitate toward the media that best express their ideas, forsaking the silent, inanimate, and noninteractive printed book.

Public Schools

High-bandwidth communication coming into the classroom has already proven itself in many tests. From a minisub in the Pacific Ocean oceanographers connected via live voice and video links to a classroom showed young minds the treasures of the sea "up close and personal." The students in turn were able to pose questions to these experts directly. That kind of connection would hardly be as strong if the experience were just a video or film presentation to a passive audience. Nor would the teacher necessarily be equipped to answer questions from students with the same perspective as specialists in the field.

Computer simulation stands to fill a huge gap caused by declining budgets for science equipment, while also opening the way for student interaction in other disciplines. Dissecting an electronic frog on a personal computer can teach one aspect of biology without offending animal rights supporters or overextending the budget—the same electronic frogs are dissected by hundreds of students year after year. Of course the kids will miss the ever-pleasant smell of formaldehyde, but perhaps the teacher could dissect one actual frog per semester so the kids can witness the real thing at least once.

Simulation doesn't have to be limited to the science lab; existing computer programs such as *SimCity* and *SimEarth* (Maxis) let anyone experiment with simulations of politics and finance. When classes in different schools are connected via the information superhighway, students from different socioeconomic backgrounds can work together on simulations, learning a lot more about each other's worlds. Kids in upper-income suburban schools shouldn't be taught under a glass bubble—they probably have more to learn from their counterparts in inner-city public schools than the other way around.

From home, students on the superhighway could use the same resources they use at school. Learning or experimenting doesn't have to end when the bell signals the end of class. Students could work together on projects, even if they cannot meet physically in the same place. Cooperative computing won't be the private reserve of business.

Reducing the Commuting Nightmare

In the last chapter we explored the potential benefits of telecommuting for reducing traffic congestion and pollution, while offering the possibilities of improving the quality of family life. Not every job lends itself even to partial telecommuting, nor would everyone want to participate in it. The key, I believe, is for companies to grant the telecommuting opportunity to individuals who would enjoy their jobs more with this kind of flexibility and personal control over their lives. Although induced by the 1994 Los Angeles earthquake calamity, formal telecommuting programs offered to businesses by Pacific Bell appear to have staying power, with 90 percent of new telecommuters continuing to work from home or satellite offices eight months after the quake (and many months after some major freeways had reopened).

Telecommuting is not *the* answer to overcrowding during commute hours best it can only delay what seems to be inevitable gridlock—or exodus of industry from congested areas in order to attract employees. But for many knowledge workers, telecommuting can be a genuine stress reducer, even if for only a couple of days each week.

At the same time, the work day's hours could spread out across the clock. With so much communication taking place on a deferred basis (voice mail, electronic mail), the need for contemporaneous meetings could drop a bit. The work day may not be a straight eight-hour shift from 9 A.M. to 5 P.M. Instead you may have the luxury of doing your creative work whenever you are most creative: at first light, midday, or nearing midnight. A potential downside, of course, is that employers and colleagues may make you feel as though you're "on call" twenty-four hours a day.

Is It Safe?

If you feel secure in your home and less so on the open road or shopping mall parking lot, then perhaps the information superhighway will let you experience parts of the outside world without having to leave the comfort of your own home. Some of today's CD-ROM multimedia productions offer previews of what we can expect via the information superhighway on-ramps.

Under the umbrella of virtual reality, there is little computers won't be able to reproduce for us, at least in a video monitor view. Walk-throughs of museums in distant cities should be no problem. The same for walking through a virtual store. As the *En Passant* CD-ROM demonstrates (Chapter 4), you can do everything but try on an article of clothing prior to purchasing it. United Parcel Service, air couriers, and local delivery services may benefit significantly from our ability to buy via video link almost anything we could buy in the store. Already in place is the mail-order customer satisfaction model that says you can examine goods purchased through the mail and return them if not satisfied.

Some goods consumers like to preview before they buy. For example, a recent survey of book buyers revealed that those who buy books in the bookstores like to browse through them, perhaps selecting one from several competing titles in a category. But if you could look at the table of contents, sample pages, index, and cover data on a personal computer or home TV set with the same graphical presentation as in the book, you would be able to do everything but feel how heavy the book is. Or when shopping for a toaster, you could not only view various angles of the product and read about its features, but—with the click of an on-screen button—call up product reviews from *Consumer Reports*. The mail-order catalog business has demonstrated that many consumers like the convenience of shopping at home, on their own time. A twenty-four hour toll-free order phone line puts the customer in charge of the shopping schedule.

I was dismayed at derisive comments about home shopping from Ralph Nader at an information superhighway summit sponsored in March 1994 by the Benton Foundation. True, not everyone may like shopping channels or appreciate this use of the data highway, but the massive success of QVC and Home Shopping Network reveals that these services strike a pleasant note with a significant audience. Good taste in programming is not the issue—meeting the wants and needs of the public is. Interactive electronic shopping contributes to the economy and will likely invite a wider range of people (including the largely forgotten female population) to ride the information superhighway.

Your Time Is Your Time

If there is one likely outcome among all the promises of the information superhighway, I believe it is that individuals will gain far more control over how they spend each minute of the day. That's not to say that time pressures will be reduced—in fact, they could easily increase as the technology encourages us to accomplish more each day. But the availability of goods, services, and other people's mailboxes will become a twenty-four-hours-a-day reality.

Think about an average week of your activities. Regardless of your household status (single, married, with or without children), your daily schedule is driven largely by others—your employer, school, government offices, stores, television programming, and the FedEx pickup deadline. Even your leisure time has a clock whose hands are run by others at theaters and ball parks, in the golf clubhouse, and on television.

In a world in which information, organizations, and people are connected to each other by the data highway, a number of aspects of our lives rigidly scheduled will become looser, able to be dealt with any time of the day or night. You won't have to wait until you reach the office to fax a sketch of an idea to a colleague—nor does the colleague have to be in the office to receive the fax. Instead of waiting for 2:00 P.M. to take a video course from the local junior college, you'll be able to use the television or personal computer at home to dial up today's video lecture for your private showing at 3:18 P.M., when you're ready to sit down for an hour. Don't have time to get to the mall before the stores close to buy a gift for a friend's housewarming party? Use the video screen to browse through several stores right now. If you make your selection early enough, it can be shipped in time for delivery the next day. (FedEx will always have a deadline, I guess). On Saturday evening, renew your driver's license from your two-way television, which can capture a photo of you at the same time—no missing work to wait in line at the Department of Motor Vehicles. Gather the family together in front of the TV set and dial up a pay-per-view movie to start right now, or watch last night's *Nightline*, which you forgot to tape.

Granted, most of these examples require the design and installation of services that are, at best, in testing stages in tiny pockets around the country. And I don't believe consumers place a dollar value on their time—at least not one that would justify extra expenditures for these services, especially if cheaper or free alternatives are available (such as going to the video store to rent a tape for less money than it would cost to dial it up from a set-top box). But assuming these potential interactive services cost the same as the alternatives, I strongly believe that being able to set your own schedule would offer a compelling reason to participate. We've come a long way from gathering around the grainy black-and-white set every Tuesday night at 8 o'clock to see Uncle Miltie.

The 80/20 Rule

I'm not sure who came up with the 80/20 rule, but it comes in handy to explain how the information superhighway will eventually integrate itself into the lives of virtually every citizen in modern society. For this discussion, I'm looking at the technologies associated with the information superhighway and their current impact on our daily lives.

The 80/20 rule theorizes that the average American—an amalgamated being, to be sure—shares a common experience, culture, and set of expectations; these common elements comprise 80 percent of any individual. The remaining 20 percent is what distinguishes one person from another—education, economics, personal experience, health, and so on.

As Americans, at least some consumer technology is common to us all and thus falls into the 80 percent classification. The voice telephone, radio, and broadcast television are common enough experiences in our country. Not everyone may own or use all these technologies, but everyone knows what they are and what they're used for: a phone call from a relative, a music recording played on the radio, and a TV situation comedy—the content from these technologies—would fall into the 80 percent of established American experience.

Of the more recent technologies, some are in transition from the 20 percent to the 80 percent side of our shared cultural experience. If VCRs were easier to use, they'd probably already be part of the 80 percent side. Most people who use the telephone take answering machines and voice mail for granted (at least when the caller doesn't have to press too many buttons to leave a message), so these are also making the jump into the 80 percent category. Audiocassettes are already there, with compact audio discs not far behind (since you can barely buy an LP record anymore and a CD player is dirt cheap). Personal computers and fax machines have a ways to go yet. Unless PCs become easier to use and less jargon-happy, however, they may never make the transition and may even be overtaken by some new kind of device, such as the personal digital assistant or personal communicator.

Currently, interactive, high-resolution digital content is a technological frontier foreign to approximately 99 percent of the population. The other 1 percent—the innovators—are only beginning to experiment with costly, clumsy pieces of a scarcely emerging infrastructure. Thus, for the population at large, contact with these technologies, such as it is, falls into the 20 percent range that distinguishes individual from individual.

Over the long term, however, I believe that the technologies and content of the information superhighway will be as much at the core of modern society as the telephone, radio, and television. By then the content and perhaps even delivery methods may be something we cannot now predict. But I am convinced that once the highways and high-bandwidth on-ramps are in place, the content will follow. If the highway engineers build it, the content providers will come.

Will We Know It When We See It?

Earlier I alluded to a significant difference between recent product-oriented consumer electronics technologies and information superhighway technologies. Product-oriented technologies tend to have fixed goals in mind. Compact audio discs offered higher fidelity and longevity than the long-playing phonograph record or cassette tape. The cellular telephone frees its owner from having to find a pay phone to maintain communications with the wired telephone world. The list goes on.

The information superhighway is not a product, however. It isn't even one technology. The information infrastructure is like a cement slab foundation. When you look at that slab, you have no idea what will be built upon it. Within inherent limitations in the area, depth, and material of that slab, an architect can build any structure imaginable. Based on market surveys, the architect imagines what kind of building people would want right away. But over time, the demand for that building space may change. The same architects or others will remodel, renovate, perhaps even tear down and rebuild from scratch atop that slab. As the needs of the community change, perhaps heralding new zoning laws and uses for the building that didn't even exist when the slab was poured, the building will be modified to remain attractive to the community. And if the demand for the latest building design outstrips the original specifications of the foundation, that slab can be increased in area, reinforced from underneath, and improved as needed to accommodate whatever kind of building the community finds it needs.

So, with the information superhighway infrastructure, today's information architects propose what kinds of data will attract the community to the highway. Through test marketing, the architects are trying to determine what data the community will want to use and how it will use it. Over time, however, the community will demand other kinds of data services. Very likely it will identify needs that today's information architects cannot predict. But tomorrow's architects will respond by remodeling, renovating, and perhaps replacing their services with ones to keep the community coming back for more. And if the community needs more data than the original infrastructure was designed to handle, that too can be arranged by widening and deepening the structure to accommodate those increased demands.

In the end, there is no end. Today's plans for video on demand, individual access to an Internet-like web of computers, virtual reality entertainment, and wireless personal communicators are founded on today's ideas of the future. We've seen enough *Popular Science* fantasy magazine covers over the years to recognize that accurate predictions of future technology and of how consumers respond to new technologies are only exercises in extrapolation of the current state of the art. When in 1968 we watched Stanley Kubrick's *2001: A Space Odyssey*, the United States was on the brink of landing an earthling on the moon only six years after the first man flew in space. It seemed fully plausible, therefore, that thirty years later we could have a commercial space station circling the Earth, complete with a Hilton Hotel, Howard Johnson's restaurant, and videophone booths, as well as extensive moon bases. Who would have thought that the United States and the Soviet Union would start to run out of money to pay for the political one-upmanship that had engendered the space race? Or that the giant Pan American Airways, proud carrier of Commander Floyd to the space station, would disappear in a puff of dust before space stations evolved beyond overgrown tin cans?

I hesitate, therefore, to view any future talk about the information superhighway as a prediction or even a vision. Rather, I see the highway as something that everyone involved—the infrastructure designers, the data architects, and consumers—can imagine. We still need the dreams to initiate such gigantic projects associated with the highway, from increased worldwide fiber-optic cabling to the sprinkling of communications satellites in our skies. As the ultimate benefactors of these dreams, we must be careful not to rely on visions of the future as hard-and-fast predictions. That way, if outside influences such as economics, politics, environmental concerns, or even our own desires alter the outcome, we will not be disappointed. For despite what predictors expect us to want from the great information superhighway, we as consumers will tell them in no uncertain terms if they are correct. And as we grow more comfortable with the broad potential of these technologies, we will be in an even stronger position to imagine what we will want next.

CHAPTER SIX

The Dark Side

If you read too many high-tech company press releases or news stories based on those releases, you can easily be lulled into a sense that the future will be rosy. We'll all be dancing merrily around the Maypole of digital telecommunications and computer technology, tra-la. The trouble is that if we're not careful about recognizing the potential hazards of the information superhighway, we consumers may become like H. G. Wells's *Time Machine* Eloi people of the future, unwittingly bred as fresh meat for the cannibalistic Morlocks—the denizens of the underworld.

At the root of the potential hazards is the fact that as individuals we essentially become digitized each time our actions touch the information superhighway. Every credit card transaction, phone call, e-mail message, digital radio transmission, product warranty registration card, real estate transaction, medical procedure, vehicle and license registration, census form, mail-order purchase, and check-written payment you generate contains information about you. That information is usually valuable to someone else, who may pay for it along with similar information on millions of other individuals. Moreover, once this information is digitized and stored on a computer somewhere, that data is potentially open for theft or modification without your knowledge.

Harm could come to an information superhighway traveler in any of several forms. A major concern is the right to privacy, which is not a globally recognized right. Another is outright theft of personal information, such as your credit card account number, which could disrupt your financial well-being until the theft is discovered and cleared up. With the digital world also representing you in the form of e-mail messages and voice mail, mischievous or evil impersonations could get you in trouble. Also, if you become part of virtual communities on-line, you may encounter the same kinds of deviants and scam artists that exist in the un-connected world. Let's examine each of these areas to understand where the threats are and what can be done to minimize them.

Privacy

Because of the power of computers to gather, sort, and analyze vast quantities of information, the perceived threat is that when a great deal of our day-to-day activity takes place on the information superhighway, we'll be sitting ducks for those entities (like governmental agencies and by business interests) that may want to track our every move. Perhaps more frightening is that a lot of that already goes on even if we're not personally plugged into the highway.

If you want to raise your paranoia level several notches, read *The Naked Consumer: How Our Private Lives Become Public Commodities*, by Erik Larson (Penguin). While researching the book, journalist Larson posed as a direct-marketing company president who was on the prowl for new customers. He quickly uncovered how easy it was for anyone to obtain mailing lists of consumers who demonstrate the most specific kinds of behavior. Your name gets onto those lists from any activity you perform that will eventually reach a computer. The simplest actions to track are credit card transactions and mail-order purchases (including magazine subscriptions). You've certainly experienced the phenomenon yourself. If you've ever purchased products from a catalog or special offer that came in the mail, you end up receiving future mailings not only from the same company, but from other companies with a similar customer base.

This probably explains a lot of solicitations. For example, a few years ago my house was listed for sale through a local office of a national real estate company. Before long I received phone calls from several moving companies who were all too happy to bid on our moving job. I had never heard from them before, nor did I hear from them after taking the house off the market.

While such invasions of privacy already exist, with increased activity on the information superhighway we'll be supplying more consumer data to the marketers along the way. They'll conceivably know what TV programs we watch (and when), more about our shopping habits if we shift some in-store shopping activity to in-home shopping, what kind of information we like to retrieve, who our friends and families are, and much more. At the same time, there may be times we want to be made aware of offers in product areas we're genuinely interested in. Hobbyists in any field, for instance, usually can't get their hands on enough related catalogs, product literature, and special offers. But when an information superhighway supplier of your video fare records information that you not only play an interactive adventure game, but also watch pay-per-view adult movies, you won't be able to tell the supplier to reveal your patterns only to video game marketers and not to adult entertainment vendors. Eventually you'll get solicitations from both the Game Channel and the Smut Channel.

Not Just Big Brother

Despite the sense that there is one huge Big Brother out there monitoring all your activity, the reality is somewhat more fragmented—many Little Brothers are on the prowl for households and bodies that fit profiles that most closely match their target audiences. The information superhighway's most effective Little Brothers will monitor your every move not only on a delayed basis (for the quarterly mailing, for example), but potentially on a daily or minute-by-minute basis. No, they won't be dropping catalogs into the mail every day, but they'll have other ways of reaching you—via the same communications links you use to exchange information on the information superhighway.

A precursor to this kind of monitoring can be seen in the operation of the supermarket checkout stand coupon-generating machine. When I buy a product at my local supermarket (an outlet of a large regional chain), the checkout clerk runs the package past the bar code scanner. Not only does that product appear on my receipt (clearly identifying the product name, size, and price) and in the store's inventory computer, but the computer prints on the spot a cents-off coupon for a store brand of the same product or another product from the same manufacturer. Had I paid for these groceries with a credit card or bank debit card, theoretically the product's maker could gain access to my address and send a follow-up mailing with offers on other products in its product line. This is target marketing at its finest: the company puts its offer into the hand of a real customer who buys the kinds of consumable products that the company sells.

On the information superhighway, marketers will know when you access a particular entertainment or information vendor. If your highway access provider displays advertisements on its screens (like Prodigy), the ads will be tailored to your on-line patterns. If you like to read *Time* on-line, then the *USA Today* folks will try to lure you their way—they know you're a news junkie and might like the daily dose of quick-hit news. These marketers will also know your e-mail address from the on-line service provider, so they may send you a message, urging you to take a free preview of some service on-line. Even if your access provider doesn't have obvious advertising space, its sign-on screen may post items of interest according to your typical on-line patterns or user profile (filled out when users sign up for a service).

Just as it is with today's information wagon trails, there will be no way to avoid being tracked—short of suicide. Some safeguards are in place now, but they don't really plan for the future. For example, the Direct Marketing Association lets consumers place themselves on lists of people not to be solicited by mail or phone. If you don't want to be flooded with catalogs and automated calls, smart direct marketers really don't want to waste their time and money contacting you. Some direct marketers are also sensitive to the privacy issue yet want to remain a part of your life if you've purchased from them before. Therefore you may sometimes see a checkbox on an order form that lets you tell the company whether they can rent your name and address to other companies that sell complementary products or services. Unfortunately not all mailers and telemarketers subscribe to the DMA's lists or respect the privacy of their customers.

The same goes for the product warranty registration cards you mail in for appliances and other goods. A manufacturer's warranty is valid whether or not you send in the card. In truth, the company is more interested in capturing your name and address so it knows its customers. As a creator of products (books), I often wish my publishers had the names and addresses of readers so announcements of new editions or related titles could reach these current customers; surely that would be a more effective marketing strategy than hoping they visit the bookstore, hear word-of-mouth recommendations, or see an advertisement. Even if the publishers did this, they, like any other marketer, would not be stalking you. Your name and address would be merely one among many—a commodity to be used, rented, and sold without your express knowledge.

Encryption Controversies

Although I see Little Brothers posing a larger threat to privacy, most of the attention lately in the telecommunications industry has been on Big Brother: the Federal government and law enforcement. At issue is a data encryption technology that elements of the U.S. government would like to force on the telecommunications industry.

First of all, data encryption is a good thing, if not a necessity to protect any consumer from potential theft and abuse of valuable personal information on the information superhighway. By jumbling the bits we send along the highway so that certain information (such as our credit card account number when we purchase goods electronically) can't be intercepted and easily read by opportunists or cyberthieves, data encryption systems ensure that a piece of data intended for an individual reaches only that individual; conversely, the recipient is assured that it was you who sent the data.

Encryption schemes are built upon complex mathematical algorithms. The way most schemes work is that the participants in a transaction (actually, their computers) have both a public and private key that are mathematically related and can unlock the encrypted data. When a sender encrypts a message with the recipient's public key, the receiving computer may unlock the message with its private key and the sender's public key. Successful decryption occurs when a message reaches only the targeted recipient, and in the process identifies the sender and verifies him or her as legitimate. As long as users keep their private keys truly private, it is extremely difficult (never say "impossible") to decrypt the message without one of those keys. Some encryption programmers are so confident of their schemes' security that they call them *digital signatures*, where computer code replaces the validity of an original human signature.

The various law enforcements agencies of the U.S. government are concerned that crooks might encrypt their communications, making it impossible for these agencies, even if they have sufficient evidence to obtain a legal wiretap warrant, to capture the meaning of data they intercept. Terrorists, the government says, could talk on digital cellular telephones or send electronic mail via commercial services to plot attacks—right under the noses of the wiretapping law enforcement agencies. The government's solution is to mandate a specific encryption scheme for which it maintains a master key (also known as a back door).

Developed by mathematical and encryption wizards in the National Security Agency (NSA), a specific encryption technology (called Skipjack) has been designed into a silicon chip that is to be part of telephones, fax machines, and computer modems. Known as the Clipper chip, this minuscule sliver of technology has won the hearts of much of government and law enforcement. Not, however, those of the general populace who are aware of these goings-on.

A number of solid arguments line up against the Clipper chip mandate. For one, criminals sophisticated enough to care about encryption will find other ways to encrypt their communications. Moreover, if the Clipper encryption system should be cracked (an engineer at AT&T has already found some chinks in the Clipper chip armor), all equipment installed with the Clipper hardware would be worthless for any kind of encrypted transactions—including everyday consumer activities involving computer passwords and financial account numbers. Should a software-only encryption system be compromised, it can be changed without having to scrap the hardware. From a global business point of view, any U.S.-made equipment that contains the Clipper encryption standard would find few customers outside the United States. Not many countries would want to rely on an encryption standard to which the United States holds the back door key.

Perhaps the most compelling reason the user community opposes the Clipper chip scheme is its mistrust of the government. Describing the Clipper chip to civil libertarians or longtime computer network aficionados causes their hair to stand on end. Stories of the government operating in heavy-handed ways against suspected computer criminals (such as confiscation of all equipment, whether or not it was part of the alleged crime) and abuse dating back perhaps to the McCarthy hearings justify the fear of putting so much power in the hands of government. One proposal from Clipper chip advocates suggests dividing the back door key into two parts, each maintained by a separate entity (either two separate agencies or one inside the government and one on the outside). The only way the keys would be released for use is with a signed wiretap warrant. In theory this system avoids the possibility that one agency with the key might abuse its power.

Americans, in particular, treasure their right to privacy. When that privacy is threatened by covert activity of the government—especially if it is discovered later that such activity was illegal—we tend to stand up and wave the Constitution. Not only do we not want anyone snooping on our private conversations, we don't even want the possibility to exist. In a poll conducted by *Time* magazine and CNN for the March 6, 1994, issue of *Time*, two-thirds of the respondents valued their right to privacy more than the ability of law enforcement to legally tap the phones of suspected crooks. An even greater percentage opposed the Clipper chip idea. While we may ultimately agree to give up some privacy rights in the name of public safety—wearing seat belts in the privacy of our own vehicles, going through metal detectors at airports—at the moment we seem to want to keep our communications private.

Privacy at Work

On the job, electronic mail and voice mail computers have also posed threats to privacy. From corporations to the basement of the White House, electronic mail archives have often been used against employees when investigations of improper or illegal behavior unearth the electronic correspondence. What makes people less cautious when communicating on computer? Perhaps they believe that, unlike typed paper memos, e-mail messages are no more than transitory characters on computer screens. Or perhaps the fact that a password is required to access an e-mail system gives them a sense of privacy. Unfortunately for the notion of privacy, electronic mail correspondence is stored in a computer just like any text document. Those with access to the computer systems have access to those messages. If compromising statements are exchanged in those messages, an unscrupulous computer systems employee or system cracker (from inside or outside the company) could use the information against the message participants.

Even the legal ramifications of expected privacy of electronic correspondence in corporate situations are still not clear. The Privacy for Consumers and Workers Act, whose intent is to spell out exactly what employers are allowed to do in the way of monitoring employee's electronic communications (and other electronic activities), has been buffeted around the halls of the Capitol without any firm action. Some interest groups—particularly those representing employers—say it's okay for a company to monitor such activity as long as the employees are made aware of the policy; others feel that electronic communications should be privileged in all cases. In the meantime, corporate e-mail is fair game for employer snooping, and commercial e-mail providers readily cooperate with law enforcement when allegations of illegal activity via e-mail arise. Therefore, until the laws change, e-mail users should not expect privacy in their communications.

Theft and Fraud

Today, long before the information superhighway is a reality, telecommunication crooks are already on the job, doing their best to rip off companies and consumers alike. From the low-tech pay phone watchers who record the credit card numbers we punch into the tone pad to the sophisticated phone hackers who intercept cellular telephone control codes and reprogram phones with stolen phone IDs, opportunities for crime exist even on the information wagon trails.

The more we allow our personal computers, cable set-top boxes, and personal communicators to handle transactions involving money, the more vigilant we must be to protect our assets. Digitization of wireless voice communications and encryption of digital signals on any conduit can help reduce the potential for information theft. But saying that these technologies will make interception impossible is like claiming to have found a mountain that is impossible to climb. Because the mountain is there, mountain climbers will try to climb it; because those technological challenges are there, hackers will try to overcome them.

Computer fraud and hacking are not necessarily one and the same. Hackers often penetrate computer systems just for the fun of doing it. Only when the information they retrieve is used against its rightful owners or when penetration of the system causes the computers to malfunction is malicious hacking—*cracking*—considered fraud.

The computer password is the weakest point of defense against unauthorized access to what you may think is your private world. Today, the common methodology for gaining access to any kind of computer—a commercial on-line service, a corporate voice mail system—is to supply two pieces of information. One is the public access name, such as your electronic mailbox address. The other is what is supposed to be another sequence of numbers and/or letters that only you know: your password. When you connect to a computing service, the main computer knows who has connected only by public identification name. In other words, if someone else should log on to the computer with your public name and your private password, the computer has no way of knowing it's not you in person or that the caller is operating a personal computer other than yours. Anyone impersonating you on the system could send inflammatory electronic mail, leave defamatory conference postings, or conduct illegal activity—all in your name. Therefore the only way you can prevent anyone from accessing the computer in your name is to keep your password to yourself.

Password Hassles

Passwords cause plenty of problems for people, especially those who have not used computers much before. First, the tendency is to use a password that you won't likely forget. If you forget your password, you'll be denied access to the system and will have to go through a lengthy verification process on the phone or via mail with the host system to establish a new account or password. As a result, one common mistake is to use a name or number sequence that is not only familiar to you, but can also be cracked using any number of public reference works. For example, many users assign the name of a child, spouse, or friend as the password. A cracker, however, can use his or her own computer to try signing on to the host system using your public ID and, as password, one at a time, every name stored in a database of names people give to their babies (from the little books you see at the supermarket checkout stands). Yes, it could take a while, but if access to your host computer account is valuable enough, the cracker may feel it's worth the effort (all of a ten-line computer program running continually for days). The same goes for any password that is a real word out of the dictionary. It's easy these days for a cracker to convert a large dictionary from a CD-ROM into a database of password attempts.

To make you just a bit more paranoid, consider this. If someone really wants to access a host computer in your name, even a numbering scheme might not provide adequate protection. The kinds of numbers easily remembered for use as passwords are birth dates, Social Security numbers, employee numbers, phone numbers, ZIP codes, and license plate numbers. If any of these numbers are in your wallet, marked in your calendar, or in plain view at your desk, they are not secure. If you have a photo of a dog or cat near your terminal, the cracker will assume that the pet's name could be a password to some place in your on-line world.

The Internet provider I use, NetCom On-Line Communication Services, Inc., suggests that your password contain both letters and numbers. The letters should not form words you'd find in a dictionary. Their system also differentiates between upper- and lowercase letters (not all do), so they recommend a mixture of these among the letters you use. Conscientious users also change their passwords every month or so. Therefore if a cracker should be monitoring all bits flowing through an Internet-connected computer, the password knowledge he or she obtains would be valid for only a short time. Finally, the longer the password, the better, because it takes more attempted combinations to find the right one. The result, then, is usually something that is difficult to remember but just as difficult to crack.

The more on-line services you access, the more passwords you may need. Admittedly, my experience may be more than that of the average user: I currently subscribe to four major on-line commercial services. I also belong to several other computer systems that either require a password to access or have password-protected information buried in the computer (for home shopping purposes). It would be extremely dangerous for me to use the same password for all of these services: if that password were ever compromised, I would be giving that crook access to every service he or she knows I belong to. Therefore, I must maintain a mental record of all these different passwords, none of which should be readily crackable. It's not easy being well connected and surreptitious.

What the lessons of today teach, however, is that authentication must be made simple for a wide audience to be attracted to the value-added services promised for the information superhighway. No one wants to devote a great deal of thought or energy to password management; it's hard enough to remember the personal identification number (PIN) for the ATM card! Nor will you want to use a single password or PIN number for authenticating all services, since the inappropriate capture of that number could open your entire electronic life to thievery by superhighway infojackers.

Virtual Community Deviants

There are likely members of your community, people who live on your block, or even members of your own family with whom you'd rather not have a lot of contact—for whatever reasons. Because you belong to those social groups, how-ever, you and the other members must coexist. In the virtual communities that exist today and will only grow as more people hook up to the information superhighway, you will definitely encounter members you'd prefer to avoid.

The situation actually gets a bit more difficult in a virtual community, because deferred messaging encourages some participants to say things they might not say in the real world. A report in the *San Francisco Examiner* (March 13, 1994) revealed the rare but true incidents of sinister activity on-line that emulates the behavior of real-world stalkers, sexual games players, and pornography peddlers. A few weeks later, in a separate case, a computer engineer was arrested for allegedly sexually molesting a 14-year-old boy whom he met via a commercial on-line service. On the data highway, today's text messages have no face, nor will a vic-tim necessarily understand the motive of someone with a loose screw. Moreover, children require just as much super-vision while on-line as they do walking home from school or talking to strangers driving by the playground.

On most commercial services it is difficult for subscribers to hide their true identities, even if the service allows users to change their on-screen names, often called *handles*. The handles are usually registered with the service (when the user of that handle is connected), and the on-line directory can tell you who's who—at least give you a real name or account identity. I personally don't like the ability to assume an alter ego while connected on-line, and I'm leery of the validity of information coming from someone who hides behind an alias.

All on-line communities walk a fine line between censor-ship and protecting its members from the unwarranted be-havior of others. Frequently forums are self-policing, and members will come to the moral defense of another member they believe is being unfairly dumped on. Commercial services monitor and manage some areas of their worlds more closely, as in the case of banning penny stock manipulators who have given costly false or misleading advice to unwary investors seeking on-line advice.

Considering the millions of individuals on-line these days, the incidents of truly criminal behavior are infinitesimally small. Today's on-line community does not mirror American society in all proportions, so it's difficult to say how tomorrow's on-line world will fare in this arena when a greater cross section of society is on-line. That's not to say that on-line meeting places don't have their share of otherwise harmless boors and pigheaded oafs, but it's usually easy enough to ignore or bypass those folks once you get to know who they are—just as you do the people you don't like in your real-world community, block, or family.

Censorship

Free speech and commercial interests do not always go hand in hand. On-line services attempt a balance between protecting free expression and protecting their interests (under the guise of protecting their customers' interests). Previous attempts at stifling discontent among on-line service subscribers have backfired, with negative publicity reaching the mainstream media. But censorship still exists in subtle ways in many places on line.

The people who moderate on-line forums exercise a great deal of control over what gets said on their forums. For the most part they let everything fly, although some individuals (dubbed NetNazis) exercise far more control over the forum's thread names, message content, and message tone than some users like.

More troubling, however, are instances of commercial on-line services burying bad news in the news services.

For example, when news about the alleged on-line child molester, mentioned earlier, revealed that he used America Online (AOL) as his communications medium, stories from the *San Jose Mercury News* (in whose county the arrest was made) were open for basic service viewing via AOL's Mercury Center on-line service only on the days they appeared in the paper. After that, the stories were shifted to a premium (in other words, extra-charge) newspaper library archive service. Yet open for basic search from the same newspaper are other stories dating back months. In fact, no other reference came forward in searches through any AOL news service only a few days after the incident. The experience shook my confidence in the thoroughness of the news items carried on the network. I received no reply from the Mercury Center moderator when I asked in a public message how archiving decisions were made.

It is clear, then, that we'll have to consider the sources any time we read or search for information on-line. Bogus information is just as easy to come by. For instance, the Internet newsgroup devoted to the San Francisco Giants baseball team one day appeared to have a note from All-Star and MVP Barry Bonds. Purporting to have an Internet e-mail originating address of bonds@sfgiants.com, the note thanked fans for their support. The problem was that buried in the gobbledygook of the message header was an indication that the message had actually originated at a Swarthmore College computer network. April Fools' Day on the Internet is a hoot. Therefore, not only may censorship exist throughout the on-line world, but users must be equally critical of anything that seems too good to be true. Both scenarios are unfortunate, because they undermine whatever potential benefit may come from virtual communities by forcing users to be overly cautious.

Life in a Box

One unexpected hazard awaits owners of personal digital assistants and personal communicators. Hundreds of thousands of mobile professionals today maintain their telephone directories, calendars, and notes in such devices as Sharp Wizards, Casio Bosses, Apple Newtons, Hewlett-Packard palmtop computers, and the like. While a lot of users of these devices engage them as peripherals to their desktop computers—containing copies of their vital day-to-day information—palmtop assistants such as these are often as valuable as the paper daybooks their owners used to carry. Inside these electronic worlds are names, addresses, and phone numbers of business and personal contacts. Confidential notes about business meetings and travel expense data fill many bytes of memory. Many users store a good chunk of their professional lives in these devices.

Their small size, which adds to their convenience, unfortunately makes PDAs prone to being lost or stolen. If future devices offer even more timely communications facilities, owners will rely on their stored information all the more. Therefore, if you find yourself leaning toward adopting a PDA or personal communicator, be sure the device offers two important safeguards: password protection and a way to back up the data.

Most devices today let you turn on a password system that forces anyone to enter the correct password upon turning on the device. Fail to enter the correct password after a couple of attempts, and the machine turns itself off. The only way to restore the unit to full working order is to completely erase all data stored inside. If your PDA should fall into the wrong hands, you won't want your private information to be revealed to those prying eyes. Therefore, as with on-line services, the password can once again protect you and your information.

The ability to back up stored information is vital for a couple of reasons. First, if your machine should break, it's unlikely that the information stored in it will survive the repair process; the service company may have to replace your unit or remove even the memory backup batteries to effect the repair. Second, if your PDA is lost or stolen, you can reconstruct your data in a replacement device from the backup copy.

Backups can usually be made either to a personal computer (through optional software and cable) or to a memory card that you plug into the device. The methods vary from device to device, and the ease with which backups can be made improves with each new generation of pocket device.

Gray Areas

In Chapter 4 I detailed another potential problem for the information superhighway: not so much the mountains of information that will be available, but the filters and agents we will use to help us sort through and establish context for what's out there. Naturally we will be encouraged to employ agents to cull from the gigabytes of new monthly information only that which we instruct our agent to grab, based on criteria we define.

I've stated the one fear I have about agents given these kinds of instructions: they will prevent new ideas from reaching us. We'll get into information patterns that feel comfortable. Rarely will we ever have the time or inclination to venture out of those bounds. Entirely new information topics that could spark our imaginations or even change our lives for the better will never find their way to our screens.

Related to this problem is evaluating the information our agents do find. Data will come from a huge variety of sources, including new sources, as individuals and organizations discover how easy it is to publish information on the information superhighway—and even get paid for their contributions. But how will we evaluate these sources? Will we know if we're being fed bogus information by a source whose goal is to deceive or disinform? Would a source reveal enough about itself that we could equip our agents to evaluate the sources for us before deciding whether the information is something we should see? Agent technology is at its earliest stages today, so it would be foolhardy to make any predictions about the answers to these important questions. Whatever the outcome, raw information will probably not be enough for those of us who intend to consume it. We'll have to rely on analyses of that information to help us understand what's being said and who's saying it. Early on, those analyses will be generated by people whose opinions we'll learn to respect, much like magazine or newspaper columnists and editors. But long term, some of that job can be handled by the agents themselves.

The danger in relying on agents for this sifting job, is the likelihood that we will lose our ability to think critically. Just as the electronic calculator has sapped the incentive to estimate a mathematical computation—which could help verify whether we've made a grave error on entering a number—so could superintelligent agents eliminate the human need to evaluate what they deliver to us. The more intelligent the agent, the more important it is for us to train it well.

Plenty of Potholes

Even before we get to the era of superintelligent agents, the information superhighway has many hurdles to overcome before the data riding on it reaches or leaves us in a smooth fashion. An incredible amount of engineering work and standard setting is necessary for such fundamental aspects as user interface design and data formats.

Major players in the information superhighway today want to own as many of the standards as possible. That's one reason we're seeing so much corporate posturing many years before the systems are deployed. Computer and software companies, such as Microsoft, Oracle, and Apple, believe they hold the future for much of what the consumer will come in contact with, in the form of set-top boxes, personal communicators, and the overall look and feel of the data-on-demand world we'll view on our video screens. Cable and telephone companies believe they are the ultimate gatekeepers to the information superhighway, since the data supposedly will be delivered on their networks. Wireless technology companies, such as Motorola and McCaw, see a large part of the highway being delivered on their wireless networks. Meanwhile, Hollywood thinks it holds the content of the future, with warehouses of existing material and the production facilities for new video, audio, and animation entertainment extravaganzas. A little farther north, in the San Francisco area, multimedia developers currently using CD-ROMs as the primary delivery medium foresee a time when they shall rule the content world, delivering the bulk of bits riding on the superhighway. At the same time, the publishing world centered in New York views the information superhighway as a new direct-to-consumer distribution medium not for only the current text and pictures they own, but for new ways of interacting with this kind of information. Some of these players hope to own huge chunks of the information superhighway, while others will be content to have well-established and well-visited boutiques there. But conflicting goals and technologies mean that few interests will be working with the same standards.

Concurrent with these technology developments, the business world is filled with announcements of alliances, cooperative agreements, licensing deals, and other joint operations among the companies that want to participate in building the information superhighway and its roadside stands. The largest companies, such as AT&T and Motorola, link up with so many other companies that it is difficult to keep track of all the pies into which they've stuck their fingers. Unlike a smaller company such as General Magic, which is dedicated to its proprietary technologies and is virtually betting the company on them, the big guns spread their risks across many technologies. Even if only a couple of them work out, the large companies will still own (minority) stakes in growing, lucrative concerns. At the same time, the big-name logo gets associated in the consumer's mind with the successful products and services they use every day. Therefore, when I read of a new alliance involving a small company and a huge one, I have mixed feelings with respect to the smaller company. On the one hand, it sounds good to have a brand-name partner in the venture, especially when the big partner has deep pockets. On the other hand, the big company isn't as bet-the-farm committed to the dream as the smaller company. In fact, it's not unlikely that another division of the giant company has a competing or market-confusing technology or alliance in place at the same time. For those of us on the consuming end of these forthcoming technologies, the alliances really don't mean a whole lot. Only the final product and how well it's marketed makes any difference. The best name on a mediocre product doesn't guarantee success (e.g., the now defunct AT&T Eo tablet computer/communicator).

The PC Pothole

The personal computer and all the software surrounding it represents another pothole in the information superhighway. Corporations are learning that a $3,000 computer ends up costing as much as $40,000 over a five-year period, after factoring in the money spent on software, training, and internal technical support. Providers who expect the personal computer to be the hardware connection between users and the highway's data had better recognize that computers are way too difficult to operate and maintain. We're scarcely any closer to the concept of the personal computer as an appliance than we were when the IBM Personal Computer came on the scene in August 1981. If you have a personal computer at home and use it actively, you know there is nothing else in the home that comes close to causing the amount of palm-sweating, tweaking, frustration and fear induced by the PC. On no other device do you worry about how much RAM is installed, how to upgrade a software program, how to adjust operating system files to make the latest hardware add-on work right, or how to keep your hard disk from filling up. To no other device do you commit irreplaceable information that can disappear in an instantaneous hard disk failure without the safeguard of an automatic backup system. Your VCR simply works until it no longer does. At that time you give it to Goodwill and buy a newer, more fully featured unit. The benefit and bane of the personal computer is that it is so malleable. It does a variety of things, it can grow and expand, and you usually need other stuff (how-to books or training courses) to get it to do what you want.

Cable companies, I believe, see this complexity as an opportunity and will be happy to gain a competitive advantage over telephone line information services by providing set-top boxes that are rather powerful personal computers disguised as special-purpose channel switchers and program playback devices. The cable company can update the software inside the set-top box via the cable without our even knowing it. The physical user interface could be a simple handheld remote control with about ten buttons on it. All the rest will occur on the screen, which we control with the handheld remote.

Personal communicators also have a shot at displacing the personal computer. These small devices, which are not necessarily tied to any existing PC platforms, can have interfaces of their own (like General Magic's Magic Cap user interface). Magic Cap, for instance, was optimized for the basic software built into devices adhering to a standard configuration of a personal communicator. As long as substantial communications services come on-line quickly to support the first Magic Cap devices, the interface has a chance to catch on—if the services are compelling enough.

Existing personal computing platforms have a great deal of baggage in the way of their installed base; if these devices are to play a major role on the information superhighway, they must evolve or adapt to new ways of thinking. If they fail to do so, the set-top box and personal communicator stand poised to pick up the slack.

Easy Complexity

As you can see, building on-ramps to the information superhighway entails far more than just making the connections between humans and the bits stored in a variety of places in the world. The computers and networks that will comprise the hidden parts of the highway are and will be among the most sophisticated civilian equipment in the world. The trick will be making this complexity simple enough to de-intimidate those consumers who can't even set their VCR clocks.

Those of us who grew up with rotary dial telephones had no idea that the pushbutton phones we started using in the 1960s would allow us to control a global web of telecommunications computers and networks, all from a twelve-button keypad. But that's what we do each time we dial a long-distance phone number. The hidden computers are sophisticated enough to perform most of the work for us. At most we have two additional buttons beyond the ten numerals, the star (*) and the pound (#), which supply us with even more power over local computers and features we use on those computers—call forwarding, three-way calling, voice mail, and so on.

We can only hope that when all the world's information is digitized and convertible into speech, text, animation, and video, we can manage that data with user interfaces as easy to master as the telephone tone pad. The less that the interface "faces" us, the more we can concentrate on the information we send and receive through the vast network of the information superhighway.

CHAPTER SEVEN

A Personal Action Plan

By now you have seen that the highly publicized, exalted information superhighway has a lengthy construction process ahead. Depending on where you work, attend school, and live, on-ramps may begin appearing at your door as soon as next week—or not any sooner than after the turn of the century.

More than likely it will sneak up on you despite what may seem to be interminable delays and false prophecies. That's why it's a good idea to be prepared for those on-ramps and in some cases even to help shape what the superhighway will bring to your work and life. With that in mind, I present one dozen items to put on your to-do list. These aren't so much specific tasks to accomplish tomorrow. Rather, they're thoughts and trends to keep at the back of your mind even after the on-ramps are firmly in place around you.

1. Greet each new information superhighway technology preannouncement with both an open mind and a healthy dose of skepticism.

The media messages we receive about the information superhighway are most often the result of press announcements by the companies who either are, or want to be, involved with the latest high-tech craze. Having experienced more than fifteen years of industry press releases, press conferences, conventions, and highly choreographed press announcements, I have become perhaps overly cynical about 95 percent of these events. But it makes my blood boil when I see untrained news writers—in all media—seemingly duped by the hype dished out by so many megabuck high-tech executives. Yes, we all want to believe that the world will be a better place, and if a product or service will do that for us, then all the better. But I wish these companies would not overpromise. I also wish the companies would make announcements that say something concrete.

A number of key words in formal press announcements stand out like red flags for me. Not all of my colleagues in the press may agree, but I'll share with you some of those key words and what they mean to me when I hear them.

ALLIANCE Sometimes modified with the word *strategic*, an alliance is usually an arrangement by which participants agree to share the risk and cost of some new venture. Only in rare instances do the parties have a clear goal in mind at these announcements, beyond some vacuous co-development scheme to become the foremost this or that. Alliances are usually hatched by the very top executives of high-tech companies. Frequently these execs don't have enough in-depth knowledge about what's going on in the labs deep inside their companies to fully understand how the technologies of the allied companies can work together or complement each other. Alliances make good news, because they tend to bring together spotlight-grabbing executives for great photo opportunities. Lower down the corporate ladder, managers and engineers are trying to figure out how the partners could possibly coexist. Participants' corporate cultures may be entirely different, creating problems when the organizations are formed with people from both companies who actually do the work.

Alliance announcements tend to be vague. They contain bogus quotes from the heads of the companies, written by public relations professionals and probably never even reviewed by those who supposedly said the wonderful words. Here's a direct quote from a recent release announcing an alliance that involved two huge companies:

> We believe that by working together we will be able to accelerate the introduction and growth of a new category of products and services that will enable consumers to exchange messages and information—wirelessly.

Translation: Our companies have the potential for doing something great in the wireless data world, but at the moment we don't have a clue as to what that would be.

In all fairness, under the right circumstances an alliance can work. Perhaps the most successful in recent high-tech history is the three-way alliance among Motorola, IBM, and Apple to develop the PowerPC microprocessor. For all three participants, however, the development of a next generation microprocessor family that was not part of the Intel juggernaut was essentially a do-or-die proposition, particularly for Apple and Motorola. This wasn't just a nice idea, but a critical move to propel Apple and IBM personal computers (with their Macintosh and OS/2 operating systems, respectively) into next generations that could compete strongly against Intel computers running Microsoft operating system software. The incentive was stronger for this alliance to work than most alliances you hear about.

Even though this alliance succeeded, and lived up to its dream of producing a very competitive product, I was skeptical about the alliance until sample chips started coming off the line. I tend to hold enthusiasm for an alliance in check until the combined enterprise actually produces a real product or service. The time gap between the announcement of the alliance and delivery of the results can be considerable. To companies about to announce their next great alliance, I say, "Thanks for the news about your alliances, but I'll wait until you actually produce something the world can evaluate. Until then, best of luck."

LICENSE AGREEMENT Related to the alliance, the license agreement is a formal relationship between the parties. It means entirely different things to each side of the license agreement. The licensor is usually the smaller of the two "partners," the one inventive and nimble enough to develop a worthwhile technology. The licensee is generally some giant corporation that feels deficient in one technology area and has found a cheap way to have access to a particular technology in case the market should require quick development of products using that technology. The sad part is that the smaller licensor has its entire stake bet on the success of its technology. It needs to line up as many licensees as possible, with the idea that dozens of companies will build products incorporating that technology—reaping a future revenue stream to pay back the years of hard work.

But the megacorporation licensee views this technology as just one of hundreds it has in its hands. If the market or products based on the licensed technology don't work out, it's no big deal: there are plenty of other things going on. In the meantime, the licensor's blood, sweat, and tears go for naught. In fact, it's not unusual for the giant licensees to license competing technologies in the same area or allow different corporate divisions to compete against each other. A licensee simply doesn't have the same gut-level commitment to a technology as the licensor. Therefore, whenever I read of licensing agreements between a small company and the likes of AT&T, IBM, Motorola, and comparable conglomerates in other parts of the world, I hope that the big company's products and marketing click for the little guy's technology. The odds, however, are against the little guy. Just ask the little companies—if they're still around—who licensed their personal computer and workstation technologies technologies to IBM over the years.

PLANS When a company or, worse yet, an alliance announces a plan, put on your dream goggles. Robert Burns knew this back in 1785:

> The best laid schemes o' mice and men
> Gang aft a-gley.

Often the plans are well intentioned. They may even become reality. But to announce a plan is to make a competitive pronouncement before anything concrete exists. The move may be preemptive, to catch a competitor off guard. It may also be a reaction to a competitor's plan—an instance of vapor chasing vapor.

DEMONSTRATIONS When a company assembles the press for a product or technology demonstration, it usually means that whatever it is they're showing still belongs in the lab. The purpose of the demonstration is to make unsuspecting audience members believe that the technology or product is real—when in fact it usually is far from it. Computer-related demonstrations, in particular, should be suspect. While this doesn't happen as often as it used to, the device or software being demonstrated is sometimes a mock-up of the real thing. The mock-up may be running on a larger computer under the table or backstage. Instead of communicating on a network, the demonstration is emulating the network communication all within the same computer—

thereby bypassing potential network snafus and usually running faster than things are working at the moment in the lab on a real network.

Many of these demonstrations are made so prematurely that the people who perform them must follow a very specific script of actions to take with the equipment or software. Ad-libbing is discouraged to avoid trying something that is either very unstable or not yet finished. At the time the demo is made on stage, engineers responsible for the product(s) have been up all night, working out enough bugs so that the big-shot executive who handles the gear in the demo doesn't come off like a fool (a smart exec hands over the demo to an engineer who knows where all the land mines are buried).

Product predemonstrations such as these are staged for a couple of reasons. For one, the deadlines are good incentives for engineers to reach certain milestones in their development cycles. But more important, the demonstration is supposed to scare the bejeebers out of competitors. Demonstrations are made to look as though the product or technology is final. And even if the competition knows this isn't the case, the trade journals may give enough press about something that seems to work—just enough to make customers pause before buying a competitor's product that isn't up to the latest state of the art, as demonstrated on stage. There is no fixed timetable between a demonstration and product shipment.

LAUNCH Here's a tricky word. When you launch a ship or a rocket, you're committed. The vessel you're launching exists and is on its way, for better or worse. For high-tech products, however, a launch may not represent the reality or commitment Cunard had when it launched the *QE II*. No, I've been to many a "product launch" at which the company shows the product for the first time, then says it won't be available for some months. Whether or not these marketers are intentionally screwing with the English language, they're assigning the "launch" term to something that is more of a "demonstration."

There are still instances when a company launches a product by showing to the public and shipping to dealers at the same time. Unfortunately, thanks to media reports that lend credence to a company's premature use of the word *launch*, the world ends up getting the wrong impression about how close or far away the real product is. As with a demonstration, the time between the loose-definition launch and shipping is not a fixed interval.

TRIAL OR TEST So much is at stake in building the information superhighway, and so little is truly known about what consumers want from it, that we're currently being subjected to dozens of localized trial and test programs in an effort to determine where things stand. On the one hand, the actual start of a trial (as opposed to a planned trial—see Plans) indicates that something is, in fact, working. On the other hand, it may also send the impression that the proprietary company has a good handle on the future and is in place to be first on the market with the best stuff. Unfortunately, the high-tech graveyard is filled with failed trials. Such failures typically are blamed on consumer apathy—an ungrateful populace not wanting what the companies believe is best for them. Of course, a failure truly indicates that the company didn't provide a compelling product or service.

Still, tests and trials are good, because no visionary can say for certain what the majority of consumers wants from the information superhighway, much less whether the conduits, central computers, or in-home devices are capable of handling the content we're supposed to demand. From these many trials, a number of good ideas will emerge. The bits we like the most and are most willing to pay for are the ones that will find their way onto other systems in the future.

SHIPS This is the magic word. A shipping product is no longer vaporware. That doesn't mean the product is necessarily good (or even truly polished). But it does mean that at least the innovators and early adopters can get their hands on the goods and evaluate the products and services. If they like what they buy, word will spread, volume will go up, prices will come down, and pretty soon there's a success story to tell. The consuming public can truly evaluate only finished, shipping products and services.

Despite my overt cynicism on this subject, we *need* to hear the kinds of announcements companies make about their futures. Stockholders need to know where their investments are headed. Business customers often require months of preparation to adopt a new or upgraded technology. Finally, the more outrageous the announcement, the more easily we can imagine what the future might hold. A prime example is the company backed by Bill Gates and Craig McCaw; these two visionaries have captured media attention with talk of launching 840 satellites in an effort to provide digital communications services to the half of the globe where wired communications is too costly or impossible to install. Exciting, yes? But let's also be careful to distinguish dreams about the future from reality. While many of today's public relations pronouncements may sound like done deals, only a small percentage of them will ever be realized—and those that will be may take longer than originally anticipated. Welcome all such announcements with both an open imagination and caution.

2. Don't rush out to buy the newest information superhighway gizmo unless an on-ramp is attached.

If you fall into the innovator class of high-tech consumer, you'll probably blow past this suggestion because you will buy the latest stuff no matter what I say. But if you are a bit more frugal with your gadget dollars, pay close attention to the promises made by manufacturers of various computer, telephone, and video equipment. Everyone has information superhighway fever, and many will exploit even the slightest connection in their advertising and promotional literature.

Be most suspicious about products in the personal digital assistant and personal communicator categories. Plenty of early bird consumers got caught up in the Apple Newton frenzy when it first shipped in August 1993. You could buy two models, one with a modem and one without. The modem was a separate small box that attached to one of the Newton's connectors. Unfortunately there wasn't any software that could let you connect the modem to perform any tasks other than sending faxes via wired telephone from the Newton. Several months later, Newton mail service began operation. But if you were already tied to one or more other electronic mail services, you couldn't access them from the Newton. If you wanted your correspondents to send mail to your NewtonMail account, you had to tell them what your new e-mail address was.

Even if a device says it offers access to a commercial service to which you subscribe, you need to dig a little deeper. While the statement of availability is supposed to give you a warm and fuzzy feeling that you'll be as much at home with your new gizmo as you are with your desktop computer, don't count on it. Make sure that all the parts of the service you use are supported by the gizmo. For example, the Tandy and Casio PDAs come with software that grants you access to America Online's graphical user interface service. The Radio Shack catalog entry for the Tandy Z-PDA reads as follows:

> It comes with America Online—just add a modem for access to stock quotes, online encyclopedia, plus the latest in news, entertainment, sports—even e-mail.

But if you are also active in the various special-interest forums, you'll be out of luck trying to access them from your PDA; the built-in software doesn't have an interface to give you access to those areas of AOL. What's more, because AOL is a graphically oriented service, you can't even get to the forums using a third-party, text-based terminal emulator program.

Another "gotcha" to watch out for is a commercial service that says it gives its subscribers access to the Internet. In one sense they're not lying about that, even if the only access they supply is a gateway for electronic mail via the Internet. But if you pick up any of the dozens of Internet books weighing down the computer book shelves at bookstores, you'll see there's a lot more to the Internet than just e-mail. An unfettered hookup gives users access to thousands of other computer systems, on-line conference communities of UseNet newsgroups, and the ability to read and transfer information on just about any topic you can imagine. An Internet provider such as a commercial service has full control over what parts of the Internet it allows its subscribers to access. For graphically oriented services such as Prodigy and America Online, or the graphical user interfaces available for CompuServe, it's no easy task making the Internet a friendly and inviting place. Therefore the depth of coverage offered by any commercial service will vary according to its internal content policies (it may not allow access to the sex and x-rated newsgroups, for example) and how far the service has come in designing graphical interfaces for an otherwise ugly and confusing on-line world. If you've been on the Internet, you'll know what to ask for; if not, you probably won't know what you're missing. The point, however, is not to judge the entirety of the Internet based on how one commercial service filters it.

Wireless devices, especially new two-way wireless devices, may also make promises that turn out to be too good to be true. First of all, the two-way wireless infrastructure is in its early stages of implementation. Depending on the wireless carrier a device supports, coverage may be limited to certain major urban areas. Try to anticipate where you will need the service, and find out if the service you're buying into is available in those areas. You'll definitely hear lots of promises about "it's coming," but you won't be able to rely on accurate dates supplied for the implementation. In both the wireless and on-line service businesses, one *is* is worth a thousand *will be's*.

3. Encourage competition for multiple highway on-ramps to your community.

Monopolistic utilities usually take quite a beating from their customers—often because they deserve it for making customers feel they're being taken advantage of. One issue is certain: the information superhighway is a threat to local monopolies, such as telephone and cable TV service. Each of those monopolies will be trying desperately to maintain a death grip on their little pieces of the information world. Phone companies now want new regulations that allow them to sell us information services, including video and audio data; if cable companies can't block phone companies from invading their turf, then cable will demand regulatory freedom to provide two-way, point-to-point communication, such as video telephone service.

Despite some bumps in the road toward less regulation, Congress will eventually enact laws that will make the bit business a relatively open market. Severe restrictions about what local telephone, cable, and broadcast companies can do with their infrastructures are lightening up. This will encourage all corporate participants in the information superhighway to compete with better or less expensive offerings and, more important, devote energy to creating entirely new kinds of services that would appeal to consumers.

Until the regulatory and business issues are resolved, however, individual consumers and communities will likely receive any number of dire predictions from the monopolies that feel most threatened by the upcoming competitive battles. When you receive a mailing from telephone and cable companies complaining about a bill in Congress or a Bill in the White House, exercise care in evaluating what the message is and who is sending you the message. Also, if your town is served by a cable company, pay close attention to issues that arise when the contract between the town and cable company comes up for renewal. Certainly the cable company is entitled to run a profitable business, but it would be foolhardy to accept all of the company's arguments and projections at face value. Get involved in the process within your community, and question items that don't make sense to you.

4. If a trial program comes to your community, participate in it.

One beneficial by-product of the dribbleware aspect of the information superhighway is that before service providers go crazy buying billions of dollars' worth of computers, they want to test out just what it is they will be sending out on their wires and airwaves. Dozens of tests are under way in communities across the United States. Each one is different from the others (just as the ultimate deployment of services will vary from town to town), but the participating households are playing one of the most important roles possible in the building of the information superhighway.

Textbook marketing teaches companies to find out what their customers want and how much they'll pay for it, then create that product so it sells for that amount of money. Unfortunately this model doesn't always work with new technologies. I heard one of the best examples of such a failure a few years ago at an industry conference, when an executive from IBM revealed the detailed market research the company did to design its first PS/1 line of home-oriented personal computers. I'm not sure where IBM obtained its sample of consumers, but the result of asking a low-tech crowd about what it wanted in a high-tech product was an incredibly ho-hum computer. If Apple engineers had blindly obeyed the same kind of market research in designing the first Macintosh, the machine would probably have been built around the MS-DOS operating system, which was the industry standard at the time. Sometimes, marketers and engineers have to dream together and take some risks, do something so radically new that no consumer would have ever thought to suggest it. Build some prototypes and then let consumers in focus groups or trials tell you what they like and don't like about it. Tweak the product based on that feedback, then break some ground when the product ships.

That's exactly what today's information superhighway pioneers are doing with these tests. It's impossible to ask consumers what they would like when they haven't a clue. Instead let the companies build some prototype services, put them in the hands of everyday users, and see what they use and don't use. And find out why.

Therefore, if a trial program should come to your community, be a willing guinea pig. Explore all the features. See which ones, if any, you gravitate to. Then be vocal and detailed about what you like and don't like. It does no good just to say you don't like a particular service. Perhaps you'd like it if it were presented differently; or maybe the service doesn't mesh with your personal interests. Say so. Participate actively, and you can influence not only your community's future service, but that of the world.

Bits coming down the information superhighway are far from the basic food, shelter, and clothing needs of our species. The right bits, however, could become so important to us that we *will* need them. Engineers and other creative people designing content are dreaming up these new things. We can't possibly know what we'll need from the information superhighway in ten or twenty years. But by participating in and responding to trial programs, we can help the creators dream up our future desires.

5. Participate in as many communications technologies at work as are available to you.

As described in Chapter 5, on-ramps to the information superhighway will be built first to businesses, schools, hospitals, and other areas with high concentrations of people. If you work at any of these places, you will have a chance to see what these technologies are like from a unique vantage point: someone will be paying you to try them out.

Since you can count on electronic messaging, information on demand, videoconferencing, and wireless communications reaching home or family members sometime in the future, you should take advantage of early incarnations of these technologies at work. The going may be rough at first, especially as some of the kinks are worked out. In corporate situations there often aren't the formal trials there are for consumer services. Typically a supplier unveils a new technology and sells the first versions for real-world installation. Learning from their early customers, the suppliers then improve the products for future releases, usually offering upgrades for the early customers.

As you use the technologies at work, think about how some aspects would be useful at home or among family members. Electronic messaging, for instance, could help you stay in closer touch with more distant relatives and friends, just as it does with colleagues and customers at work.

Also, if a telecommuting option is offered to you, take the company up on it, at least for a trial period. It's difficult to change habits, so the idea of not going in to the office or working from a satellite office will feel strange at first. You may feel disconnected from your colleagues, unable to keep up with the latest gossip (that's what e-mail is for!). But give it a chance to see what it means to how much you accomplish when working away from the office, or how much better you feel for not snailing your way through rush-hour traffic, or how it brings you closer to your kids and pets. I know that when I started freelance writing full time in 1981 after many years of working in traditional settings, it took me years to get over the guilt of taking a half-hour walk in the middle of the afternoon. Even though I commonly worked many more hours per day and weekends than my neighbors, I was self-conscious about taking a midday walk while normal employed people "should" be working. (I've long since gotten over that guilt and wouldn't trade the freedom for anything.)

If there is one potential downside to this ready adoption of technology at work, it is that you will associate the wonders of telecommunications only with work and will reject their intrusion into your home and family life. I hope that instead you treat technology simply as a tool to help you perform your work, with the possibility that similar tools can help around the house. Running a household these days is getting to be more like running a small business, so perhaps that represents an even stronger link. But just as a delivery van driver doesn't shun the automobile for going to the supermarket, so should you not disconnect from the information superhighway at five o'clock.

6. Avoid one-way communications technologies unless you have an overpowering immediate need.

The information superhighway cannot become merely a giant pipe of digital information flowing into your lap. There is already more information broadcast to the world than the world can absorb. To make the most out of the highway, it must be a two-way street. While we might want to receive far more than we send, we will want to send more and more stuff as time goes on—putting our agents onto the highway to search and filter for us, for example.

More important, I believe it's far better that both transmissions take place over the same conduit. As a result, I'm uncomfortable with plans for interactive broadcasts, such as direct broadcast satellite and wireless cable systems. Whatever input these broadcasters expect from you will not only be meager, but will have to come via another medium: the telephone. Such interaction may be no greater than phoning in a request for a pay-per-view movie or other entertainment event. In those cases the taps of a few telephone push buttons is all the computer at the broadcaster's end needs from a human. I suppose that qualifies as being "interactive," but it's no way to interact in real time with a program similar to the interactive multimedia you can buy today on CD-ROM for use in a personal computer. For that kind of interaction you need a permanent, high-bandwidth connection back to the source. It's unlikely that you'd want to tie up a phone line for an hour to handle the data of a multimedia program or install a separate data phone line whose only outlet is next to the cable jack.

A better two-way system uses the same phone or cable line to get data to you and from you. The more interaction on your part—not just a video game controller, but even video signals for a video phone call—the more bandwidth is needed for the connection. Those cable companies that offer pseudo-two-way service will still need to retool their systems to accommodate the larger quantity of bits you'll eventually be sending onto the information superhighway.

Wireless one-way message service is another kind of one-way communication that to my way of thinking has limited application. Packaged in gizmos ranging from alphanumeric pagers to plug-in cards for laptop computers and PDAs, these are compact radio receivers that capture messages directed to a specific device, just like an addressable cable decoder. Services for these devices include detailed text messages from your office or a paging service, as well as updates for news, stock, and sports data that are broadcast throughout the day on the special frequencies.

What I don't like about this technology is that the sender of the message never knows if it reached your receiver, much less whether you actually read the message (the receiver can store the message until you get around to reading it). That's the nature of one-way pager messaging: the message is sent through the air like a broadcast. The message contains the address of your receiver, which captures the message whenever it hears a message with its address in it. But if you should be someplace where the radio signal is blocked or inadequate, the message may not reach you.

On most systems there is at least a stopgap method that lets you know later when you've missed a message. Since messages directed to you carry a sequential number, if the number of the next message that reaches the receiver does not follow the previously received message, you get a visible alert that you missed a message. You can then call the carrier on the voice telephone to resend that missed message.

A two-way data system, however, obviates this telephone tag problem, because the receiver silently acknowledges the connection with the sending service. If the receiver isn't available, the sender can store the message and try later. Not only that, but as the message is sent (usually in short bursts of data called *packets*, which are then reassembled as a single message in the receiver), the receiver compares its error detection code against the one sent by the sender. If the codes differ, then some data in the packet got jumbled along the way: the receiver asks the carrier to resend that packet. So goes the data-only conversation between receiver and sending computer until the entire message is received. At that time, the sending computer knows the receiver has the message in its inbox. The person who sent the original message may ask the computer to send back a return receipt that provides the sender with a time stamp of a successful transmission.

Two-way wireless digital data exchanges require more in the way of portable equipment and more complex gear in the infrastructure to handle the transactions. Thus, devices like Motorola's Envoy personal communicator (first "demonstrated" in March 1994 and due to ship about the same time as this book) are not cheap, and service range is limited to where the two-way wireless networks are up and running. But the message exchanges are more assured for both parties. As more messaging and information retrieval is deemed to be "mission-critical," even for communication with family members over inexpensive devices in the years ahead, two-way messaging will be deemed essential. The more demand innovators in business applications can demonstrate for two-way digital data, the sooner the infrastructure will cover cities and vacation getaways equally—and the cheaper the service will become. Two-way wireless digital data should follow at least the same growth path as portable cellular telephones, if not a greater one.

7. Encourage government to facilitate building on-ramps to every office, school, hospital, and home.

The last thing we need is the U.S. government building the information superhighway for us. While it has already built some parts of the highway, from here on it's best left in the hands of private industry, which can react more quickly to technology advances and is in a better position to deal with consumer marketing and the development of services that consumers will want.

Private industry still needs help from the government, however. First, restrictive regulations need to be lifted. A number of these regulations have twisted histories, some dating back to the Communications Act of 1934 and some coming as an outgrowth of the breakup of AT&T in 1982. The AT&T breakup, in particular, came about from the perceived fear that the telephone line into homes could become a noose around the consumer's neck, providing the sole source for not only voice telephone calls, but also information services (few of which existed in those days). In the intervening years, technology and the business structure of the regional Bell operating companies have improved the consumer's lot in some regards, but not enough to satisfy forward-looking policymakers. They now see that it's better to allow an even playing field for multiple carriers to compete for all types of communications.

More important help is needed, however, to give private industry either the rate structure or other government-sponsored incentives to make sure the map of the information superhighway includes all socioeconomic pockets of

America. As mentioned in Myth #6 (Chapter 4), the need for universal service is widely acknowledged among policymakers. We must make sure they don't forget their promises.

Defining universal service for the information superhighway is extremely difficult. Access to the highway is only one aspect of what the highway is all about. What good is an on-ramp from a household that would be considered part of the "have-not" group of our society if that ramp leads nowhere of interest to that constituency? Since no one has a totally clear picture of what services will be available on the highway when the on-ramps reach 60 to 80 percent of households, there certainly is no vision about what would constitute universal service. It's hard to imagine defining video on demand—a currently fashionable service to tout—as a lifeline service. Nor can universal service possibly be "universal": whatever may flow on the highway, the MIE needs of the inner city will certainly be different from those of a farming community. In today's world, about the most visible icon to all communities is McDonald's. Perhaps there will evolve the data equivalent of a McDonald's on the information superhighway. Or it may be more like Burger King, where it's okay to "have it your way."

Some of today's information highway trial programs are being criticized because they appear to be delivered only to middle- and upper-income communities. The charge of "redlining" has even been leveled against some regional phone companies for their choice of test locations. I believe much of this concern is misplaced. For one, if there is to be universal service, it must be subsidized by those who pay for enhanced services—the very services being tested now.

If enhanced services cannot be well enough defined to attract paying customers, there will never be funds to provide universal service to anyone. Moreover, I have yet to hear solid suggestions for the content that is to be included in universal service, so what is there to test in lower-income communities? While we definitely cannot forget universal service, it's premature to claim that trial programs are guilty of discrimination when they themselves are groping for definition.

These are crucial times in establishing the information infrastructure. Write to your representatives in Washington about how you feel about the need for accelerated wiring of our nation. You can also make your feelings known by supporting groups such as the Electronic Frontier Foundation (155 Second Street #35, Cambridge, MA 02141) or Computer Professionals for Social Responsibility (P.O. Box 717, Palo Alto, CA 94301), both of which are dedicated to promoting democratic uses of computers and communications technology. Their executives frequently testify in congressional committee hearings, and their views are taken into account by members of the executive branch as well.

At the local level, another potential roadblock is looming. Utility companies engaged in wiring our communities will often have to dig up streets and tie up traffic in the process. Such is the case in Milpitas, California, where Pacific Bell wants to lay fiber-optic cable throughout the town for future services. The city government, however, wants more than $1 million to cover its projected costs of early road improvements (digging up a street shortens the life of the existing pavement) and the myriad other hassles that the construction would cause.

Also at stake is the portion of cable TV subscriber fees that the cable company now pays to the city. Pacific Bell's anticipated service will include video programming that competes against the existing cable TV operation. But since Pac Bell doesn't need a cable television franchise agreement with the city, it doesn't need to pay such fees. How this dispute ends will influence the speed with which on-ramps will be built around the country, especially since it is unlikely that on-ramp builders will be able to afford such payments to every city on top of their costs of doing the work.

My belief, however, is that on-ramp construction can only enhance a community in the long term, making the city more attractive to businesses and families with school-age children. If your town is involved with this kind of concern about on-ramp construction, participate actively in the discussion to help the parties reach conclusions quickly.

8. If you own a personal computer at home, sign up for at least one commercial on-line service.

While a personal computer is not the be-all, end-all access path to the information superhighway, it can provide a glimpse of some of the possibilities that will be exploited even further when the wagon trails to our homes (plain old telephone system lines) are paved and widened into genuine highway on-ramps. You certainly won't be alone. The subscriber bases of all the commercial services are climbing steadily.

It would be presumptuous for me to recommend a service for you. I don't know your potential areas of interest; you don't know all of my interests. But you can find a service that feels right for you by one of two methods: asking friends who are not only on-line, but also share your interests; and taking up some of the services on their free trial offers.

With so many computer owners now accessing commercial services, you may have friends or relatives who already subscribe to services. Ask them what parts of the service they use, how they like the people they encounter, and what their monthly bills tend to be. While you can exchange e-mail with virtually anyone who belongs to any service, including the Internet, there may be surcharges for messages transmitted outside your own service. Therefore, if you intend to communicate with family and friends via e-mail, select a service they use.

If your computer is a Macintosh or it runs Microsoft Windows, I recommend services offering software that provides a graphical user interface to their systems. Prodigy and America Online and any new service that starts up these days require a graphical user interface. Older services, such as CompuServe, Delphi, and GEnie can be used with a straight text-based terminal or with optional graphical front end software. The graphical software hides the complex command structure of the innards of the system. In the case of CompuServe's special-interest forums, for instance, the CompuServe Information Manager software (available for Macintosh and Windows) makes it very easy to follow discussion threads and know when someone has responded specifically to a posting you've made in the forum.

Should you go onto the Internet? If you're new to on-line communications, the Internet may overwhelm you with its complexity and vastness. Depending on how you connect to the Internet world, you may have to learn a bit of the Unix operating system and file management, which is the antithesis of the friendly interfaces of Windows or the Mac. I think a better choice would be to join one of the consumer-oriented services, such as America Online or CompuServe, that offers Internet access via a graphical user interface. On the other hand, if someone knowledgeable can set you up with an Internet account and with graphically oriented software, you might give the Net a try. The one sense you get from coursing through the Internet that you don't from the commercial services is that of internetworked computers in locations around the world. At first you may feel like an unauthorized hacker gaining access to a computer system located at some university or government entity—

even though that computer was designed to be accessed by the Internet public.

Whatever your choice of on-line access, begin by exploring the system to which you subscribe. Don't be afraid to join special-interest groups. There is rarely any extra charge beyond the hourly rate, and joining is a mere electronic formality. Then do lots of reading of things on-line. Get to know some of the forums and their participants by reading their message threads. You'll often see messages to or from someone called a *sysop*. That's on-line-speak for system operator—the moderator of a section. That person tries to keep the threads labeled properly so folks like you can follow conversations if you begin reading one from somewhere in the middle. On most services, each forum also has libraries of computer files related to that topic. Browse through the summaries of those files—even download one to your computer if you can figure out how (instructions are usually available for reading right from the libraries). In addition to the community forums, pore over the information sources to see if they have the coverage and depth you'd like for news, weather, travel, and reference material. After a while the software and your excursions should begin creating a mental model in your head for the service in general. That's a good sign that you're beginning to feel comfortable within that service.

Be aware, however, that even with the latest services, the bulk of the information that moves in real time between the host computer and your own is in plain text. As more bits can flow between the two machines with faster modems or future all-digital connections, text will be enhanced with more graphics, sound, and even video. The e-mail you leave on tomorrow's systems may be not a text message, but a videogram, recorded from the small video camera built into the top of the video monitor of your computer and sent to the on-line service as you record it. We're a long way from reaching that stage, but today's services will prepare us for a lot of innovation that will come along with the wider bandwidths to our homes.

9. If you don't own a personal computer, don't rush out to buy one just to jump on the information superhighway.

In all my years of writing about personal computers, this is the first time I've recommended holding off on a personal computer purchase. This recommendation is directed primarily to consumers who have no experience using a business-level personal computer, such as an IBM-compatible or Macintosh. My sense is that if you've had an overwhelming perceived need for a computer at home, you probably already have one, regardless of vintage. And if you've kept up with the machine, using it frequently for any purpose ranging from games to taxes, then you have also probably gone through one or more episodes of utter confusion and frustration when something didn't work as you expected. For instance, upgrading to a new version of the machine's operating system may have rendered some favorite programs inoperable; connecting an external peripheral, especially on an Intel-based machine, took hours, if not days, to accomplish correctly; trying the latest interactive multimedia CD-ROM disc under DOS or Windows required tweaking operating system files consisting of gibberish. And these are the users who know that there is no "Any" key.

The problem isn't that today's personal computing newcomers are less technically sophisticated than their predecessors; the problem is that the computers haven't gotten any easier to manage and maintain, despite a number of user interface improvements. Manufacturers are trying to make things easier, but the progress is slow. Without question, the Apple Macintosh makes computing life simpler, largely by taking care of otherwise complex issues, such as connecting

CD-ROM drives and extra hard disk storage devices or adding memory. I don't like technology to get in my face when I'm trying to write an article, manage my finances, send an e-mail message, or win a game. Even though I have a good handle on Macintosh operations, I shouldn't have to call upon that expertise to get through the day. After growing up on DOS (beginning with the first IBM Personal Computer in 1981), many years ago I switched my primary production computer to the Macintosh. I still believe it's an easier environment in which to learn. Independent studies of computers in business use also back up that assertion. Yet my colleagues and I still write books to help new and intermediate users learn the Mac and get out of jams that afflict all personal computer users. Regardless of brand, personal computers are more complicated than they need to be.

If it were a simple matter of buying a desktop information appliance that let you subscribe to and dial up a commercial on-line service of your choice, I would make that recommendation to the non-computer-equipped individual today. Unfortunately no such gizmo exists. Your choices are to go whole hog with a general-purpose personal computer or try your hand at one of the new personal digital assistants, which come closer to the information appliance idea. Since you may feel compelled to see what this highway business is all about, I can at least provide some guidelines to help you decide what to buy.

Once you decide to buy a regular personal computer, the biggest choice you'll have to make is the *platform*. For home-based computing, there are two mainstream choices: an Intel-based machine or an Apple Macintosh.

Intel is the name of the manufacturer of the central microprocessor chip inside the majority of personal computers sold today. But that's just the box. What gives the computer it's personality is its *operating system* software. Intel boxes are typically sold with Microsoft operating system software (although some IBM-brand computers come with IBM's own operating system software, called OS/2). The Microsoft operating system, called MS-DOS (Microsoft Disk Operating System), has an optional, friendlier on-screen presence called Windows. A newer version of Windows, to be available in 1995, combines the functions of DOS and Windows into a single graphically oriented operating system.

Apple is in a unique position in that it designs both the hardware boxes and the operating system software. Since its debut in 1984, the Macintosh has benefited from this tight integration by letting the operating system software handle more of the complex hardware chores for the user. Also, Apple instilled user interface guidelines on software providers, which gives users of all programs a common way of performing similar tasks, such as storing data and printing documents.

Whatever the differences between platforms (major application software is available for both), your choice should actually be based more on which platform has the most help available to you. Even though the Macintosh might be easier to learn and upgrade, if all your friends have DOS/Windows machines, they won't be able to help you much if you have a question about managing printer fonts.

A second recommendation is to purchase personal computing systems that come preconfigured and loaded with basic software right out of the box. Macintosh Performa models come this way, as do DOS/Windows machines from IBM, Compaq, AST, and others. Large computer retailers (superstores) and consumer electronics chains tend to carry these configurations, because they want to sell the simplest possible solutions. Electronics stores salespeople may know even less than you do, so take your time to browse, ask your knowledgeable friends for help, and tread carefully. Laptop and notebook computers are also good out-of-the-box solutions.

My third and final personal computer recommendation is not to leave the store without a telephone modem. For years I've believed no computer should be sold without a modem, but then I've also been a longtime believer that a personal computer is predominantly a communications device for which the telephone line is an important input/output route.

You'll get a lot of conflicting advice about modems—whether they should be internal or external (I recommend an internal or plug-in-slot-based modem for laptop/notebook computers), how fast they should transfer data, and whether they should do fax sending and/or receiving. For most of today's commercial on-line services, a 2400 *bps* (*bits per second*) data modem works adequately. Fax capability (at 9600 bps, rated separately from the regular computer data transfer rate) is usually available for very little extra money and is definitely worth it, at least for sending fax messages from the computer. In the future, however, the services will be wanting to shuttle more information to you to enhance those services (with graphics and even video). Faster modem speeds will be needed to accomplish this. Most commercial services have 9600 bps dial-up service available in larger cities, with a few offering even faster access at 14,400 bps (unfortunately they often charge more for the faster access, which in my view makes no sense since faster downloads of files allow more callers to share the same system resources). You need good-quality voice lines to maintain connections at 9600 and 14,400 bps, and the local phone calls you make to access commercial services in metropolitan areas can usually handle the load. Therefore I recommend getting as fast a data modem as you feel comfortable affording. A 14,400 bps modem should get you through the next couple of years in good shape. By then, new standards and faster data rates will usher in new generations of modems.

So much for personal computers.

One reason I like to think about recommending a communicating PDA for newcomers is that PDAs don't carry all the historical baggage that personal computers do—they're not weighed down by aging operating systems and user interfaces. Of course a PDA doesn't do (nor is it intended to do) everything that a personal computer does. You're not going to write the great American novel on a PDA, nor will you perform massive financial analyses on one. A PDA is a smaller-scale device, intended to help you manage personal information, such as your telephone directory, schedule, to-do lists, and other notes. Better PDAs allow you to add software from other companies that extend their ability to manage your predominantly mobile life.

Should you choose the PDA route, be sure your device includes not only a modem, but software (built in or available from third parties) to connect with the on-line world. The ability to participate in electronic mail should be your first priority. Virtually any e-mail service provides a gateway to the Internet, so the e-mail address you give to others would be the Internet equivalent. Among the first PDAs to be designed specifically for communications are those employing the Magic Cap operating system developed by General Magic. Sony's Magic Link Communicator started shipping in September 1994. Additional devices from Motorola (the Envoy has been "demonstrated") and others should be shipping at various points throughout 1995. On-line services are in the very early stages of working with Magic Cap. At&T PersonaLink offers powerful agent-aware e-mali service. America Online provides the same abridged service for Magic Cap devices that it provides for Tandy/Casio PDA devices.

Admittedly, access to some on-line services via PDA can be problematic when the user is required to input a lot of text (as when participating in discussion forums or even composing e-mail). While corresponding with another Magic Cap device is as simple as sending a handwritten note via the network, such notes won't be converted to anything that a CompuServe e-mail user could read. Typewriter keyboards built into small devices aren't easy to use for extended typing by experienced touch typists, whether the keyboards are physical keys or on-screen representations. Therefore, look to communicating PDAs as predominantly read-only devices (for longer text sent by others) and for sending only short notes. Regular personal computers, or external keyboards for PDAs, are better devices for extended textual input.

Because so much of the intended infrastructure for wireless PDA communications is in the construction stage, at this time I recommend wireless PDAs only for the innovator and early adopter categories of consumer (who may treat such devices as peripherals to their desktop computers anyway). Prices will be comparatively high at first, and new generations of devices will come along quickly. The next three years will be heaven for gadget freaks.

10. Devise ways of contributing to the information superhighway.

By "contributing," I'm not talking about stringing your house with fiber-optic cable or buying a video-on-demand server for your school. The most important contribution that individuals can make to the information superhighway is in the content that roars down the lanes.

All those quadrillions of bits stored on interconnected computers around the world don't mean anything without human intelligence to interpret them, converting raw data into information and knowledge. You may not be a computer or telecommunications expert, yet you still have expertise in areas that are of value or assistance to others in virtual communities that live along the information superhighway. Each of us has something to contribute to these communities.

Even in its wagon trail stage, the information superhighway today offers outlets for ideas. While the mechanisms for collecting royalties for on-line works are still being worked out, you are free to pursue fame and recognition by publishing your writing and art in designated places among the thousands of on-line libraries of similar works. With the natural selection afforded by special-interest forums within on-line communities (on both commercial and Internet systems), you can direct ideas to audiences more highly targeted than any direct marketer could hope for.

I suspect that entrepreneurs will find ways of more formally publishing electronic newsletters on very narrow topics. With virtually no up-front costs in marketing, printing, or mailing, such newsletters should grow into interesting businesses for individuals who would otherwise not have the wherewithal to start up a publishing venture. Payments may end up being handled in numerous ways. For instance, with an up-front payment to the on-line carrier for a particular newsletter, issues are e-mailed to subscribers the instant they're finished. Alternatively, the on-line carrier could pay the newsletter author/publisher a royalty based on the number of downloads or readings of the newsletter—coming out of the on-line service's regular subscriber billing.

And if you're not comfortable creating information on your own, there are plenty of folks in the virtual community who can use your help. Communities surrounding hobbies and life experience already abound on local bulletin board services as well as on international commercial ones. Community members feel free to post questions in public with the hope that another member has an answer, recommendation, or consolation for whatever concerns the petitioner. There is no other way to help so many people without having to leave the comfort of your home. On your first visits to special-interest communities, you may feel intimidated by the knowledge of other longtime members. Soon enough, however, you'll encounter questions to which you have the only or best answers. Each member of a virtual community has much to contribute. The collective knowledge of community members scattered throughout the world of internetworked computers is almost frightening.

11. Demand intuitive access to the information superhighway.

A lot of creative people are spending hundreds of millions of dollars to produce the reasons we will want to ride the information superhighway. By and large, the pioneering developers are experimenting. It's difficult for them or anyone to predict what the consumer base will want and how much consumers will pay for it. Still, content providers must start somewhere, producing prototypes and early products that we can adopt and reject to reveal our own unknown tastes and expectations.

A crucial role for all consumers—especially the innovators and early adopters—is that of vocal critic. If, as so many of us have done with personal computers, we put up with sloppy or confusing user interfaces, complex mental models of systems, and unengaging material, we'll be sending the message that mediocrity is acceptable. Because users did that with DOS computers, for instance, a large portion of the installed base for personal computers thirteen years later is struggling through simple tasks, such as intelligently naming a hard disk file with only eight characters. Innovators and early adopters, unfortunately, tend to put up with a lot of inconvenience and poor design to be first on the block with the latest gadget. The burden is heaviest among these consumer segments to tell providers of hardware and content connected to the information superhighway what's right and wrong with their creations.

One important customer relations value that the computer software industry can impress on the entertainment and publishing industries is the readiness to fix problems. Dedicated users have an amazing wealth of forgiveness when a company blows its first product but makes great strides in producing a terrific second version. Left to their own devices, producers outside the personal computer software industry might not reflect those values and could, instead, blame failure on the customer rather than on their products or services. This is one vital reason that the telecommunications, cable, entertainment, and publishing companies should have partners from the computer industry.

The more experience you as a consumer have with technology and computer communications, the more you must strive to *turn off* that knowledge when introduced to a new product or service. Other consumers further along the adoption curve won't have the same expertise or patience you have, so you can do the most good by "down-teching," and see a) if you can use whatever it is without poring over a manual or summoning your high-tech knowledge; and b) whether the offering not only engages you the first time, but makes you want to come back for more at a later time.

There's a good chance that if you're reading this book, you are an innovator or early adopter. While I hope that constituents from other portions of the technology adoption curve and journalists from all camps are also reading along, I charge the innovator and early adopter with the responsibility of shaping the future of the information superhighway. Dollars from these groups will be doing the most talking early on. Support and talk up those products and services you believe meet stringent criteria of ease of use and value; reject jargon and acronym clutter; alert producers of the not so good about what's wrong; and give them suggestions about how to fix the problems. The exchanges between providers and consumers will be much like a tennis game. Providers serve the ball; after that it's up to both parties to respond with respective volleys to keep the point going. The minute consumers let a volley pass them by, they'll be stuck with the current technology: chance of further improvement and development will be lost forever, and the world will be saddled with a standard that's an insult to the technological abilities of its creators and to the desires of its users. The key, I believe, is reminding providers that consumers own the ball and can shut down the game before the provider has a chance to win the game, set, or match.

The more we demand excellence from content providers, the more quickly they will race to meet those demands and resist getting in a rut that could hinder development in the future. Insist on being personally enriched from the highway. If the technology cannot make complex parts of our lives simpler and make our existence more fulfilling, then all we've done is create a world of dead-end alleys instead of high-speed superhighways. We may never again have this opportunity to shape so much of our future.

12. Prepare for and accept change.

Fear of the unknown is scary enough when there's always the chance that the present will carry you through and everything will be all right. More frightening still is when the future guarantees change. I believe if anyone feels threatened by the information superhighway and all it entails, that fear is based on the knowledge that the good old days will probably never return.

Well documented is the recent transition in the United States from an economy influenced strongly by heavy industry to one whose strength lies in information and service. Rust Belt industry employment has shrunk, forcing many blue- and white-collar workers to retrain for careers they had never thought about. When an economy in general fluctuates, the workforce faces massive displacement, as the most recent U.S. recession has demonstrated. No company or industry is safe from the twists and turns of politics, economics, or technology.

A strong message comes out of this turmoil—a message that is tough for some to take: From now on, change will be the constant. The individuals best prepared to succeed are those who can learn, modify, and grow, regardless of age, experience, or ego. The days of working for the same company from graduation to retirement are long gone. So may be the days of having the same career over that period. Employment uncertainties during the recent recession surely caused many workers to wonder about a company's commitment or loyalty to its employees. Since long seniority or high performance reviews didn't necessarily prevent the ax from swinging in a lot of companies, workers might feel as though they're on their own, even while employed. Who knows? Perhaps if everyone has guaranteed access to health care, the workforce could one day consist entirely of independent contractors. Farfetched for today, but it drives home the point that we are increasingly dependent on our own efforts for our futures. Career success will be measured by how well each of us can adapt, adopt, and become adept at whatever is thrown our way.

Information superhighway technologies that will both accompany and hasten our journey into the future will themselves be changing radically and quickly. If you've already been participating in the personal computer or cellular telephone segments of today's information wagon trails, you've probably witnessed—or fallen victim to—technology advances that made still new products seem obsolete before the warranty ran out. It's rare to peruse an on-line forum specializing in a particular kind of computer equipment after the release of some faster, lighter, smaller, longer-battery-life gadget without seeing several flames written by customers who bought the previous model just last week. They feel betrayed, lied to—all kinds of persecution and paranoia flow.

As long as there are willing customers for the latest technologies, the makers of the goods will keep updating their designs in an effort to remain one step ahead of the competition. Hardware manufacturers in particular are doing whatever they can to reduce the time between product introductions, only occasionally providing upgrade options for their current customers. While painful for many consumers to accept, information superhighway hardware products you buy will likely be replaced by more desirable versions within less than twelve months; possibly within five years the device may not even work if it cannot be upgraded or modified to coexist with changes in the highway infrastructure (such as reallocation of radio frequencies for a wireless service).

On the software side of the street, upgrades are already a way of life in personal computers. Consumers are demonstrating some backlash against the rapid pace of upgrades coming from so many of their software suppliers. For now, the pressure to upgrade to the next version—which is usually more complicated thanks to added features—is not as great as it used to be. Software vendors are finding that more customers are sticking with versions that they know work and do the job. And that only forces the companies to produce new versions offering even more compelling reasons to upgrade.

Personal computer software is only a tiny proportion of the software and other content that will fill the information superhighway. The more tightly integrated a device's software is to the service it works with, such as a set-top box, the more transparent the upgrades will be—they can be done over the cable, wire, or air without your having to do more than tap a button to approve the automatic upgrade.

More important, though, the nature of all content on the highway may evolve into areas that don't exist today. Clever marketers will listen closely to how consumers respond to early offerings; clever engineers and multimedia designers will dream up new ways for individuals to communicate and expand their minds. Constant evolution and occasional small revolutions are sure to be the mainstay of life along the information superhighway.

The better prepared we are to accept change, the less terrifying those changes will be. The information superhighway will be about change and will be changing, itself, in the process. All the better to create the next generations of earthlings who will accelerate the process even more in search of the good, simple, and fulfilling life.

GLOSSARY

Information Superhighway Glossary

Many of the buzzwords for the information superhighway have meanings that originated in other times and places. In this glossary, however, I focus on the meanings as they apply to the information superhighway and all its appendages.

address In electronic mail terms, the unique combination of letters, numerals, and punctuation marks that identify a mailbox on a computer network. When the network is connected to other other networks (as on the Internet), part of the address may include the identifier for the computer network to which the addressee belongs.

agent For telecommunications, a software program that performs processes on behalf of a human user. The telecommunications system must include a computer that knows how to run the agent program, usually while the human user is disconnected from the computer network. An agent may gather information and send it to its human owner via an electronic mail message.

alliance An agreement among two or more corporate entities to develop and/or market a technology together to share the costs and risks. Announcement of an alliance does not guarantee that the joint effort will come to fruition or succeed.

ATM Asynchronous transfer mode, a method of passing digital data (at very high speeds) from computer to computer. Information is divided into labeled chunks (called *packets*), which are commingled with other packets along the connection. At the receiving end, the packets are reassembled into their original order and sent to their final destination. There is no relationship between asynchronous transfer mode and the automated teller machine.

backbone A major electronic corridor for data along a network, generally operating at high speeds. A backbone might contain data formatted according to the ATM protocols.

back door In computer security terms, a usually secret password known only to the agency or individual who sets up the password security system. An unscrupulous or disgruntled former employee, whose authorized access is canceled upon termination, has been known to use the back door to access the employer's computer for personal gain and/or sabotage.

bandwidth The measure of how much data flows through a conduit. Usually measured by how many bits per second can flow through a wire, fiber-optic cable, or radio link. In more casual senses, bandwidth may include resources on a computer network ("Don't waste bandwidth sending flames to this idiot") and an individual's apparent diversity of knowledge or ability to work on many different things at one time ("He's a high-bandwidth kind of guy").

binary A counting system containing only two possible numerals: 0 and 1. Also used to describe issues that appear to be simple yes-no, black-white decisions.

bit A contraction of "binary" and "digit," the smallest piece of data that can be stored or conveyed by a computer. Usually represented by either a zero or a one.

bps Bits per second, the number of bits conveyed along a conduit within one second.

byte A grouping of eight bits. Because an eight-bit binary number provides enough combinations (256) to represent each letter, numeral, and punctuation mark of all roman alphabets, the byte is a common measure of computer storage capacity: one byte equals one recognizable character. Common quantities for personal computer storage today are thousands of bytes (kilobytes, KB), millions of bytes (megabytes, MB), and billions of bytes (gigabytes, GB).

CD-I Compact disc–interactive, a format for storing digital data on an optical disc that looks like the audio compact disc. CD-I discs are read-only and used primarily for entertainment devices designed specially to accommodate the format of the data on the disc.

CD-ROM Compact disc–read only memory, a format for storing digital data on an optical disc that looks like the audio compact disc. Used commonly for distributing multimedia and information archives, CD-ROMs themselves usually come in versions designed for a particular kind of computer system (such as personal computers running Microsoft Windows; the Apple Macintosh; Sega Genesis; and so on).

CDPD Cellular digital packet data, an emerging standard for allowing wireless devices to send digital data using the existing cellular telephone network. CDPD requires the installation of compatible equipment by the cellular phone carrier to accommodate transmissions from a portable computer or PDA that is sending data formatted for CDPD. The portable computer or PDA must also have a CDPD-compatible modem on its end. CDPD contrasts analog methods of sending audible modem signals over standard cellular phone links that require no enhancement to the cellular carrier's equipment.

Clipper chip An integrated circuit that contains the U.S. government–engineered Skipjack encryption software. Some government agencies recommend building this chip into all telecommunication products to ensure that digital communications are encrypted for privacy as well as to allow authorized government and law enforcement agencies legally to wiretap and decrypt digital communications. Opponents fear a lack of true privacy and other potential hazards.

content The generic name given to the information delivered via the information superhighway or other media (such as a CD-ROM).

cracker A hacker whose goal is to gain unauthorized access to computers and networks. Some crackers do it for the challenge presented by computer security systems. Others do it to obtain private information, plant bogus information, infect systems with damaging computer viruses, or commit other malicious acts.

cyberspace The virtually unmappable web of interlinked computers and networks, including public areas such as the Internet and commercial services. The term was coined originally by William Gibson in his science fiction work *Neuromancer.*

data Raw streams of bits that flow through a conduit or are stored in computers. When converted to human readable/audible/viewable form, data becomes information.

DBS See *direct broadcast satellite*.

dial-up A connection to another computer by way of the standard telephone line. A dial-up connection usually requires a telephone modem on both ends of the line.

digital A method of conveying information in the form of bits. Real-world analog information (sound and video especially) needs to be converted electronically into digital form to be sent as bits.

digital convergence A convenient phrase depicting the manner in which a variety of information types (text, sound, animation, video, graphics) can all flow through the same conduits once the information is converted into digital form. The term also refers to the various information-providing industries, whose boundaries increasingly overlap as their content is converted into digital data (for example, publishing and computing industries working together on CD-ROMs).

direct broadcast satellite A wireless information delivery vehicle that sends one-way television, radio, or digital data signals from an artificial (orbiting or stationary) satellite to ground-based receivers in the home.

dribbleware My term for technologies and products that are deployed or released unevenly over a long period of time and in varying degrees of completion.

e-mail See *electronic mail*.

electronic mail A method of exchanging messages among individuals using a computer or computer service as the delivery and forwarding mechanism. Each electronic mail user has a virtual mailbox on the main computer that stores incoming messages until the user retrieves them by way of a personal computer or PDA.

encryption A method of scrambling information so that only the intended recipient can unscramble the data. Information is encrypted with one key and unscrambled with either the same key or a complementary key, known only to the participants in the message exchange.

ENIAC Electronic Numerical Integrator and Computer, generally acknowledged to be the first electronic general-purpose computer. Demonstrated publicly in 1946, ENIAC contained 18,000 vacuum tubes and required a 30- by-50 foot room to enclose it. The computer was designed originally to calculate ballistic missile trajectories.

FAQ Frequently asked question, often the name of a file or message on a bulletin board or Internet UseNet newsgroup that covers the basic questions most newcomers have about the subject.

fax Short for facsimile, a method of communicating a visual image or document from one point to another via telephone or radio signals.

fiber optics A data communications medium that sends information in the form of light pulses over very thin glass fibers at very high speeds.

filter In electronic mail systems, a program that allows a user to designate which received mail messages should appear in the in-box. A filter compares the message title and name of the sender of all incoming messages against lists prepared by the recipient. Some filters also act as agents by forwarding or responding automatically to messages as instructed by the recipient.

flame On bulletin boards, a message containing written attacks against individuals, organizations, or ideas.

flamer An individual who posts a flame to a bulletin board.

ftp File transfer protocol, one of several standards, primarily on the Internet, used to transfer data files from one computer to another as a way of copying files to your own personal computer.

gateway A connection from one computer network to another. The most common gateways are those that allow users of one electronic mail network to exchange messages with users on a different network. Communication among networks is controlled entirely behind the scenes for the user.

gopher An Internet software service that helps users locate and transfer downloadable documents and other files scattered around the Internet.

hacker A dedicated computer user who enjoys digging deeply into how various parts of a computer or computer network operate. Although the term carries a negative connotation because of improper media coverage (see *cracker*), a hacker usually tries to make improvements to hardware and software systems without resorting to illegal or unethical means.

infobahn One of many mass-media synonyms for the information superhighway.

information Raw data that, converted into forms that a person can read, see, or hear, conveys knowledge.

information superhighway An amorphous communications network of computers and conduits, envisioned as a system that allows individuals equal access to the world's knowledge at any time from anywhere. In practice, the information superhighway will consist of many different networks carrying some unique and some overlapping information services, available on an uneven basis around the world.

interactive multimedia A presentation of information using a combination of static (such as text and graphics) and time-based (sound, animation, video) media that also encourages the user to participate in determining the content. Most interactive multimedia programs are delivered today on CD-ROM and CD-I discs. As the bandwidth of communication conduits leading to homes, schools, and offices increases, more programs will become accessible via cable, phone lines, and wireless networks.

Interactive Network A pioneering company based in Sunnyvale, California, that produces largely one-way wireless interactive programming to a special in-home console. Signals to the home consoles are broadcast as a hidden part of a local television station signal. Users can play along with some television game shows and sporting events. Return information is handled over the telephone after a telecast.

Internet A worldwide collection of computers and networks formed originally as a messaging and information-sharing network for government scientific researchers. Unlike a commercial service on-line, the Internet does not have any governing organization. Longtime users have established an on-line culture that is not tolerant of unsophisticated newcomers and commercialization. Nevertheless, the information-routing facilities of the Internet are used by thousands of academic, government, and business computers daily.

ISDN Integrated Services Digital Network, a digital communications standard established by Bell Labs to facilitate sending higher bandwidth data on standard telephone lines than can be sent with traditional analog voice communications. A number of versions of the ISDN standard now exist, some capable of linking multiple ISDN data channels into one capable of handling full-screen color video and sound.

kbps Kilobits per second (thousands of bits per second). See *bps*.

key In encryption technology, a sequence of numbers used to mathematically encrypt and decrypt digital information. The same or mathematically related keys are required on both ends of the communication to convert the encrypted data back into its original form.

LAN See *local area network*.

launch In technology marketing, a publicity event signifying a milestone for a product or technology, ranging from first public showing to actually shipping. The precise definition varies with use.

license agreement A formal agreement between two or more technology parties whereby one party pays the other for use and/or manufacture of a technology. The licensee generally pays a fee (onetime or royalties) for use of the technology.

Little Brothers My term for the various electronic monitors of an individual's activity on the information superhighway. Such monitoring of usage patterns will be used primarily for demographic data gathering for future direct marketing promotions aimed at users meeting certain demographic profiles.

local area network A connection of two or more personal computers, allowing an exchange of data or shared resources (such as printers, fax modems). Most LANs require physical wired connections among users, but recent technology also allows for wireless connections within a school, office, or home.

Mbps Megabits (millions of bits) per second. See *bps*.

MIE My term for "messaging, information, and entertainment," the three broad categories of content flowing along the information superhighway.

modem A device that converts a computer's electronic digital signals into audible tones for transmittal over standard telephone or wireless telephone connections. The same device on the other end demodulates those audible signals into digital signals that the computer uses.

multimedia A presentation consisting of static (such as text and graphics) and time-based (sound, animation, video) information.

Net, the A term used casually to refer to any part of the on-line world, including, but not limited to, the Internet.

netiquette The unwritten laws of courtesy and cooperation among users of the Internet or any commercial on-line service. Violators often receive flames to alert them to their transgressions.

NetNazi A heavy-handed (sometimes self-appointed) moderator of a bulletin board group, who exerts excessive control over the content of users' messages, message names, and organization.

newsgroups The bulletin board groups of the Internet. Collectively, newsgroups belong to a global network called

UseNet, which handles how messages are routed among the world's Internet sites.

on-line The status of having your computer or PDA connected to another computer via telephone, network cable, or wireless connection. After disconnecting, you are said to be off-line. Service software that lets you compose and read messages off-line can lower the cost of using a service, which generally charges for the number of minutes you are on-line.

on-ramp A metaphor for the way an individual connects to the information superhighway. The on-ramp may be the TV cable, a telephone line, or a radio signal, depending on the devices the user has or the services to which the user wishes to connect.

operating system The computer software program that instructs the collection of chips and other devices in a computer to behave as it does. All machines that are run by the same operating system (such as MS-DOS 6.21, Macintosh System 7.5) behave the same way and can use the same application program software (word processors, spreadsheets, graphics, whatever). Even closed devices, such as set-top boxes and PDAs, have operating systems, which start up when the user turns on the device.

optical fiber The hair-thin glass thread that conveys vast quantities of digital information in the form of light pulses.

password A sequence of letters, numbers, and/or punctuation symbols used as a key to allow a user to access a computer or network. A password should be kept private and secret by the user to prevent anyone else from accessing the computer in the guise of the authorized user.

PCS Personal communications service, a new class of wireless communications that will supplement the cellular telephone system. Predictions include lower cost for both the telephone (lower power required) and service. Implementation in the United States requires allocation (via lottery) of frequencies to service providers.

PDA See *personal digital assistant.*

personal communicator A variation of the personal digital assistant whose application focus is on communications. A personal communicator comes with at least a telephone modem built in; more expensive models come with wireless modems.

personal digital assistant A handheld and/or pocket-size device capable of storing and displaying digital information. Current models focus on personal information applications (calendar scheduling, phone directory, note taking). Customized software for PDAs is designed for specific professions, such as medicine or others with mobile applications. Some PDAs include a modem (or have a connector for one), while others do not. The palmtop computer category also falls under the PDA umbrella.

POTS Plain old telephone service, the standard voice telephone line that comes into residential or pay phone installations.

protocol A set of rules governing the format and transmission of information among computers. A protocol can turn into a standard protocol either by industry agreement or by common usage.

RBOC Regional Bell operating company, also known as a Baby Bell, one of the seven regional companies formed to handle local telephone service in the United States after the court-ordered breakup of American Telephone & Telegraph (AT&T) in 1982.

sampling The process of taking an instantaneous reading of a signal and converting that reading into a digital number. For example, typical compact disc audio sampling consists of 44,100 samples of the sound each second. Once in digital form, the data can be reproduced accurately and transmitted without degradation.

server A computer-controlled device (usually a computer itself) that acts as a centralized information warehouse to which other smaller computers (clients) connect. Depending on the purpose of the network, a server may contain an electronic mail processing facility, reams of shared information, or other information that is to be disseminated gradually to each smaller computer that comes on-line.

service provider An individual or company that distributes information via the information superhighway. Services may range from one-way broadcast to interactive systems, such as electronic mail and bulletin boards or multiplayer entertainment over a network.

set-top box The cable convertor device that today connects incoming television cable with the TV or VCR. As envisioned for digital services of the future, the set-top box may include a hard disk for temporary storage of downloaded movies or other video entertainment.

Skipjack The encryption algorithm developed by the National Security Agency (NSA) of the U.S. government, to be built into the Clipper chip.

smiley A series of punctuation symbols and other text characters used to convey emotion in text-only e-mail or bulletin board messages. The term comes from the original symbols, :-), which, when viewed by tilting the head ninety degrees to the left, looks like a smiling face and conveys the writer's smile.

switching The technology of connecting one signal source to a single recipient. Used primarily in telephone connections today, switching, which is accomplished at the utility company's computer, may invade the delivery of video information over cable television, displacing the current cable broadcast method.

technical support The assistance available to users of high-tech products. Also known as *product support*, technical support may be offered by a product company (hardware or software) via telephone, e-mail, mail, or fax. Some companies provide unconditional free support, while others have varying programs of free and/or paid support.

telecommuting Performing work away from the primary workplace with the aid of telecommunications technology, ranging from voice telephone to computer modem to video-conferencing. Telecommuting may be from one's home, hotel room, or satellite office set up by the company to reduce employee commuting.

telnet An Internet service that allows users to connect directly with a specific computer connected to the Internet. Some computing systems grant access via gopher, while others use the telnet protocol.

thread In bulletin board messaging, the sequence of messages pertaining to a topic defined in the message's subject field. Some bulletin board services organize threads such that browsers can follow the precise sequence by a visual map of messages and responses.

trial A test program established by an information utility to measure customer receptiveness to a new service. A trial is usually limited to a small geographic area, such as the reach of a community cable television system.

universal access The concept of providing information superhighway access to all citizens, regardless of socioeconomic status.

UseNet The aggregate of computers and their interconnections that comprise the bulletin board services of the Internet. Each bulletin board subject area is called a *newsgroup*.

user interface The point at which a human and product meet. In personal computers, the user interface is the computer's on-screen persona, which determines how the human user controls the computer and responds to its actions. Microsoft Windows, OS/2, and the Macintosh provide graphical user interfaces, meaning that information stored in the computer is represented by recognizable on-screen objects (such as file folders or disk icons). All machines made to be used by humans have user interfaces, such as the twelve push buttons of the home telephone and the dashboard of an automobile.

vaporware A product or technology announced by its producer prior to its availability to its intended audience.

virtual community A group of individuals from geographically diverse locales who electronically exchange ideas and messages with each other on subjects of common interest. The computer bulletin board is the most popular meeting place for members of a virtual community.

WAN See *wide area network*.

wide area network A number of interconnected local area networks, which are spread over a large geographical area. Very common in networked corporations with multiple facilities.

wireless cable A one-way information distribution system, primarily of video services, broadcast to a metropolitan area and providing the kinds of video programming normally delivered on wired cable systems. A wireless cable receiving setup includes a special antenna and set-top box.

INDEX

A

Access to the information
  superhighway, 103–5
  access to government
    and, 106–8
  intuitive, 212–14
  literacy and, 105–6
  universal, 200–202
Advertising, 58–59, 160–61
Agents, software, 124–28,
  174–75
Alliances between
  companies, 176–77,
  182–83
America Online (AOL), 172
Analog data, 12
Animals! (CD-ROM),
  99–100
Animation, 100
Answering machines,
  28–30
Apple Computer, 101, 207.
  See also Macintosh
  computers
AT&T, 199
Audio compact discs (CDs),
  12
Audio messages, 136

B

Bandwidth, 13
Banking via telephone and
  personal computer, 139
Bell, Alexander Graham, 4
Bell Laboratories, 13
Big Brother, 160–62
Binary system, 11
Bits, 11–12
Bits per second (bps), 13
Blackmail (film), 55–56
Books, on-line access to,
  146–47
Browsing, 127–28
Bulletin boards, 94

C

Cable television, 25–26,
  46–49, 66, 73–76,
  201–2. *See also* Set-top
  boxes
  five hundred channels
    of, 136–38
  interactive, 74–75,
    196–97
Cable TV companies, 178,
  192

California Department of
    Transportation
    (Caltrans), 109
Catalogs, on CD-ROM,
    101–2
CD players, 115
CD-ROMs, 15, 99–103
    First Person series of, 101
Cellular modems, 112
Cellular telephones, 18–19,
    39–40, 112
    pagers vs., 38
    roaming, 118–19
    standards issue and,
        118–19
Censorship, by commercial
    on-line services, 170–72
Change, preparing for and
    accepting, 214–17
Channel surfing, 46–47
Claris Corporation, 61
Clipper encryption system,
    163–65
Commercial on-line
    services. See On-line
    information services
Communications satellites,
    118–19
Communications
    technologies. See also
    specific technologies
    one-way, 196–99
    at work, 194–96
Compact disc–interactive
    (CD-I), 99
Compact discs (CDs), 53–54
Companies, 176–77. See
    also Alliances between

companies; Service
    providers; and specific
    types of companies
    demonstrations by,
        185–86
    license agreements
        between, 184–85
    plans of, 185
    product launches by,
        186–87
    shipment of products by,
        188
    trials and tests of
        products by, 187–88
Competition among
    companies, 62–63,
    65–67
    for multiple highway
        on-ramps to your
        community, 191–92
Computer fraud, 166–67
Computer Professionals for
    Social Responsibility,
    201
Computers. See also
    Personal computers
    digital information and,
        11–12
    Macintosh, 206, 207
Conduits, 16–19
Congress, 9–10, 192
Consumers
    innovators and early
        adopters, 114–15
    targeting, 119–20, 159–61
Contributing to the
    information highway,
    210–12

Forums on commercial
on-line services, 44–45,
95–97, 170–71. *See also*
Virtual communities
Fraud, computer, 166–67
Fremont, California, 107

G

General Magic, 124
Gore, Albert, Jr., 8–9, 88,
92
Government, 52
access to, 106–8
role in building
on-ramps, 199–202
Government Printing Office
(GPO), 107
Government regulations,
9–10
Graphical user interfaces,
70
for on-line information
services, 203

H

Hackers, 166–67
Handles, 170
Highways, 2–3
Hitchcock, Alfred, 55–56
Home shopping. *See*
Shopping
Hughes Aircraft Company,
119
Hypertext linking, 129

I

IMHO (in my humble
opinion), 135

Information, 19–21
electronically published
(on-line), 20–21
Information overload,
121–22, 128, 130
Information providers,
20–21. *See also* Service
providers
Information publishing, on
commercial services,
97–98
Information superhighway,
x–xi, 1. *See also specific
topics*
advertising on, 58–59
construction of, 52, 53
financing of, 56–57
infrastructure of,
154–56
as metaphor, 2–3
myths and
misconceptions
about. *See* Myths
and misconceptions
about the
information
superhighway
potholes in, 175–78
tolls for access to, 57–58
transition to, 51, 55–56
Infrastructures, 144–46
Innovators, 114–15, 116,
189, 212, 213
Interactive cable TV, 74–75,
196–97. *See also* Set-top
boxes
Interactive entertainment
services, 79–81

competition among,
65–68
distinguishing among,
68–69
Services, 66–68. *See also*
Service providers; *and
specific types of services*
overlap among, 67
Set-top boxes, 15, 16,
73–76
standards problems and,
116–17
Shipment of products, 188
Shopping, 149–50
previewing before
buying, 150
Shopping, interactive,
101–2
Signatures, digital, 163
Simon communicator, 84
Simulation, 147–48
Skepticism
toward new gadgets and
services, 189–91
toward technology
preannouncements,
181–88
Skipjack (encryption
technology), 163
Smileys, 135
Solicitations, 159–61
Standards, 116–17,
175–76
Supermarkets, 160
Switches, telephone, 5
Sysop (system operators),
204

T

Tandy PDAs, 189–90
Target marketing, 119–20,
159–61
Technical support, 71
Telecommuting, 110–11,
148–49, 195
adapting to, 111
Teledesic, 119
Telegraphy, 4
Telephone answering
machines, 15
Telephone companies, 17,
191
Telephony (telephone
communications), 4–5.
See also Cellular
telephones
fiber-optic cables and,
14–15
wiring, 24
Telescript, 124, 125
Television, 7. *See also* Cable
television
Tests and trials of products,
187–88
Theft, 166–67
Threads, 44
Three-dimensional space,
displaying information
in, 129–30
Time, saving, 113, 151–52
Transportation
infrastructure, 145
Travelers, wireless
technologies for,
112–13

Trial programs, participation
in, 192–94
Trials and tests of products,
187–88

U

Un Do Me (music video),
80–81
Universal service, 200–202
UseNet, 86–87
Utility companies, 201

V

Vaporware, 54
VCRs, 115
Videoconferencing, 8,
109–10
ISDN standard and, 14
Video displays, 77–78
Video messages, 136
Video on demand, 138–40
Virtual communities, 20,
68–69, 130–33
deviant members of,
169–71
Virtual reality, 149
Voice mail, 28–30

Voyager Company, 79–80,
101

W

Warranty registration cards,
161–62
WELL, the, 132
Western Union's Desk-Fax,
40
Wide area networks
(WANs), 70
Windows, 207
Wireless conduits, 26–27
Wireless data connections,
18, 19
Wireless networks, 18
Wiring, telephone, 24
Work. *See also*
Telecommuting
participation in
communications
technologies at,
194–96
privacy at, 165–66
while traveling, 112–13
World War I, 6
World Wide Web (WWW),
89, 128